First World War
and Army of Occupation
War Diary
France, Belgium and Germany

61 DIVISION
Headquarters, Branches and Services
Royal Army Ordnance Corps
Deputy Assistant Director Ordnance Services
1 December 1915 - 28 June 1919

WO95/3041/3

The Naval & Military Press Ltd
www.nmarchive.com
Published in association with The National Archives

Published by

The Naval & Military Press Ltd

Unit 10 Ridgewood Industrial Park,

Uckfield, East Sussex,

TN22 5QE England

Tel: +44 (0) 1825 749494

www.naval-military-press.com

www.nmarchive.com

This diary has been reprinted in facsimile from the original. Any imperfections are inevitably reproduced and the quality may fall short of modern type and cartographic standards.

© **Crown Copyright**
Images reproduced by permission of The National Archives, London, England, 2015.

Contents

Document type	Place/Title	Date From	Date To
Heading	WO95/3041/2		
Heading	61st Division D.A. Dir.Ordnance Services 1915 Sep May-Jun 1919		
Miscellaneous	D.A.D.O.S. War Diary For September, 1915		
Miscellaneous	War Diary		
Heading	War Diary of D.A.D.O.S. 61st Division From 1st December 1915 To 31st December 1915		
War Diary	Boicham	01/12/1915	31/12/1915
Heading	War Diary of D.A.D.O.S. 61st Division From 1st January To 31st January 1916		
War Diary	Boreham	01/01/1916	31/01/1916
War Diary	In The Field	14/05/1916	31/05/1916
Heading	War Diary June 1916 D.A.D.O.S. 61st Division B.E.F.		
War Diary	St Venant	01/06/1916	12/06/1916
War Diary	La Gorgue	13/06/1916	28/08/1916
Heading	War Diary D.A.D.O.S. 61st Division B.E.F. September 1916 Vol.5.		
War Diary	La Gorgue	01/09/1916	31/10/1916
Heading	War Diary D.A.D.O.S. 61st Divn Nov 1-30th 1916 Vol VII		
War Diary	St Venant	01/11/1916	02/11/1916
War Diary	Chelers	03/11/1916	04/11/1916
War Diary	Roellecourt	05/11/1916	06/11/1916
War Diary	F. Le Grand	06/11/1916	15/11/1916
War Diary	Bernaville	16/11/1916	16/11/1916
War Diary	Canaples	17/11/1916	17/11/1916
War Diary	Contay	18/11/1916	22/11/1916
War Diary	Bouzincourt	23/11/1916	28/11/1916
War Diary	Hedauville	28/11/1916	28/11/1916
Heading	War Diary D.A.D.O.S. 61st Division B.E.F. December 1916. Vol.8.		
War Diary	Hedauville	03/12/1916	25/12/1916
Heading	War Diary D.A.D.O.S. 61st Divn Vol IX January 1917		
War Diary	Hedauville	01/01/1917	15/01/1917
War Diary	Brailly	16/01/1917	31/01/1917
Miscellaneous	War Diary D.A.D.O.S. 61st Divn. Feb. 1917 Vol X		
War Diary	Brailly	01/02/1917	05/02/1917
War Diary	Long	06/02/1917	14/02/1917
War Diary	Guilla Court	15/02/1917	18/02/1917
War Diary	Harbonnieres	19/02/1917	26/02/1917
Heading	War Diary March 1917 Vol XI D.A.D.O.S. 61st Division		
War Diary	Harbonnieres	01/03/1917	29/03/1917
War Diary	Croix Molignaux	30/03/1917	31/03/1917
Heading	War Diary D.A.D.O.S. 61st Division April 1917 Vol 12		
War Diary	Croix Molignaux	03/04/1917	12/04/1917
War Diary	Voyennes	12/04/1917	21/04/1917
War Diary	Voyennes Auroir	22/04/1917	26/04/1917
Heading	War Diary D.A.D.O.S. 61st Division May 1917 Vol 13		
War Diary	Foreste	01/05/1917	16/05/1917

War Diary	Vignacourt	17/05/1917	21/05/1917
War Diary	Doullens	22/05/1917	23/05/1917
War Diary	Le Cauroy	24/05/1917	24/05/1917
War Diary	Warlus	26/05/1917	31/05/1917
Heading	War Diary D.A.D.O.S. 61st Divn June 1917 Vol XIV		
War Diary	Warlus	01/06/1917	02/06/1917
War Diary	Arras	03/06/1917	11/06/1917
War Diary	Warlus	12/06/1917	23/06/1917
War Diary	Willeman	24/06/1917	29/06/1917
Heading	War Diary D.A.D.O.S. 61st Division July 1917 Vol XV		
War Diary	Willeman	01/07/1917	26/07/1917
War Diary	Zeggars Capel	26/07/1917	31/07/1917
Heading	War Diary D.A.D.O.S. 61st Divn August 1917 Vol XVI		
War Diary	Zeggers Cappel	01/08/1917	15/08/1917
War Diary	Poperinghe	16/08/1917	31/08/1917
Heading	War Diary D.A.D.O.S. 61st Division September 1917 Vol XVII		
War Diary	Poperinghe	01/09/1917	15/09/1917
War Diary	Watou	18/09/1917	25/09/1917
War Diary	Arras	26/09/1917	30/09/1917
Heading	War Diary D.A.D.O.S. 61st Divn October 1917 Vol XVIII		
War Diary	St Nicholas Arras	01/10/1917	20/10/1917
War Diary	Arras	21/10/1917	30/10/1917
Heading	War Diary D.A.D.O.S. 61st Divn. November 1917 Vol XIX		
War Diary	Arras	02/11/1917	30/11/1917
War Diary	War Diary D.A.D.O.S. 61 Div N December 1917 Vol XX		
War Diary	Bemulencourt	01/12/1917	01/12/1917
War Diary	Etricourt	02/12/1917	31/12/1917
Heading	War Diary D.A.D.O.S. 61st Div N January 1918 Vol XXI		
War Diary	Harbonnieres	01/01/1918	07/01/1918
War Diary	Nesle	09/01/1918	12/01/1918
War Diary	Auroir	14/01/1918	29/01/1918
Heading	War Diary D.A.D.O.S. 61st Division Feb 1918 Vol XXII		
War Diary	Auroir	01/02/1918	28/02/1918
Heading	War Diary D.A.D.O.S. 61st Div. March 1918 Vol XXIII		
War Diary	Foreste	01/03/1918	28/03/1918
Heading	War Diary D.A.D.O.S. 61st Division April 1918 Vol XXIV		
War Diary	Boves	01/04/1918	02/04/1918
War Diary	Pissy	03/04/1918	10/04/1918
War Diary	Aire	11/04/1918	29/04/1918
War Diary	Aire	01/04/1918	17/04/1918
War Diary	Lambres	18/04/1918	13/04/1918
War Diary	Norrent Fontes	18/07/1918	21/07/1918
War Diary	Wardrecques	22/04/1918	30/04/1918
War Diary	Norrent Fontes	01/06/1918	07/07/1918
War Diary	Widderbroucq	08/08/1918	24/08/1918
War Diary	Tannay	25/08/1918	31/08/1918

War Diary	HQ 61 Division D A A G	01/06/1918	01/06/1918
War Diary	Grieve Farm Merville	01/09/1918	17/09/1918
War Diary	La Gorge	17/09/1918	30/09/1918
War Diary	Aire	04/09/1918	04/09/1918
War Diary	Doullens	05/09/1918	08/09/1918
War Diary	Velu	09/09/1918	10/10/1918
War Diary	Graincourt	11/09/1918	17/09/1918
War Diary	Cambrai	18/09/1918	19/09/1918
War Diary	Avesnes	20/09/1918	31/09/1918
Heading	War Diary November 1918 D A D O S 61st Division		
War Diary	Avesnes Les Auberte	03/11/1918	08/11/1918
War Diary	Bermerain	09/11/1918	14/11/1918
War Diary	Cambrai	15/11/1918	16/11/1918
War Diary	Cambrai	20/11/1918	21/11/1918
War Diary	Bernaville	24/11/1918	30/11/1918
Heading	War Diary December 1918 2 Sheets		
War Diary	Bernaville	04/12/1918	05/12/1918
War Diary	St Riquier	08/12/1918	30/12/1918
Heading	War Diary January 1919 Vol 33		
War Diary	St Riquier	01/01/1919	29/01/1919
Heading	H.Q. G Division "A"		
Heading	War Diary For February 1919		
War Diary	St Riquier	03/02/1919	28/02/1919
War Diary	St Riquier	26/02/1919	26/02/1919
War Diary	St Riquier	01/03/1919	24/03/1919
War Diary	Le Treport	25/03/1919	29/03/1919
War Diary	Le Treport	01/04/1919	29/04/1919
War Diary	Le Treport	02/05/1919	30/05/1919
War Diary	Le Treport	03/06/1919	28/06/1919

WO 95/30411/2

61ST DIVISION

D.A.DIR.ORDNANCE SERVICES

1915 SEP ~~MAY 1916~~ -JUN 1919

D.A.D.O.S. War Diary for September, 1915.

Units other than R.A. are practically complete with Vehicles.

An Eastern Command Communication has been received to the effect that the A.S.C. Officer i/c Barracks, Chelmsford is to carry out the duties laid down for a Barrack Officer. This will be of great relief to Units.

Units are now complete with Telephone Equipment to authorised Scales.

The chief items now being issued are stores under A.F.G. 1096- series to complete vehicles.

Boreham House,
Chelmsford.
9.10.1915.

Lieut. A.O.D.
D.A.D.O.S., 61st Division. T.F.

WAR DIARY
or
INTELLIGENCE SUMMARY

Army Form C. 2118

Oct 9
Sept 15

Supply of Egypt is proceeding somewhat slowly.

C.F.S. Wagons are needed for A.S.C. and R.E.

All Rs. Arms in possession of Units other than Infantry (525 each Bn nominally but then damaged since Lydd) have not been replaced though due on Establt) have now been withdrawn.

E. Phillips
Lt. A.O.D.

D.A.D. of O.S. 61st DIV

CONFIDENTIAL

Army Form C. 2118

WAR DIARY
D.A.D.O.S. 61st S.M. DIV
—OR—
INTELLIGENCE SUMMARY
From Nov 1st to Nov 30th 1915

(Erase heading not required.)

Instructions regarding War Diaries and Intelligence Summaries are contained in F. S. Regs., Part II. and the Staff Manual respectively. Title Pages will be prepared in manuscript.

Place	Date	Hour	Summary of Events and Information	Remarks and references to Appendices
			1. All Japanese rifles and ammunition has been withdrawn from Infantry units of the Division, and .303 MLE and MLM received in lieu, a report on the latter arms being now in course of preparation. Full complement of Bayonets not yet received.	
			2. The issue of complete 16 pr equipment to the Artillery has commenced, also the issue of 100 rds of Shrapnel Shell per gun.	
			3. G.S. Wagons still due to ASC & R.A. Not available at present.	
			4. Rangefinders & Prismatic Compasses are being issued to the infantry.	
			5. Equipment under G.1099 Series proceeds steadily but slowly.	
			K. Farquharson Roberts	
			Lt. A.O.D.	
			D.A.D. of O. S. 61st DIV. T.F.	

Confidential.

War Diary
of
D.A.D.O.S. 61st Division
from 1st December 1915 to 31st December 1915.

Army Form C. 2118.

WAR DIARY
INTELLIGENCE SUMMARY

DADOS
61st (S.M.) Divn

(Erase heading not required.)

Instructions regarding War Diaries and Intelligence Summaries are contained in F. S. Regs., Part II. and the Staff Manual respectively. Title pages will be prepared in manuscript.

Hour, Date, Place	Summary of Events and Information	Remarks and references to Appendices
1.12.15. Bordon	Arriving DADOS. 18 pr equipment for Artillery commences to arrive.	K.T.R.
2.12.15. "	To OR men duties as DADOS	K.T.R.
3.12.15. "	Outbreak of mumps 2/1 Glos Bde RFA. Arranged issue of regimental stores	K.T.R
4.12.15. "	NIL	K.T.R.
5.12.15. "	18 pr shrapnel shell arriving. Received letter from Central Force stating 3,000 rds of shrapnel shell despatched to the Division	K.T.R.
6.12.15. "	By GOC's orders attended Inquiry at Brentwood as to fire 2/6 Glos Regt. Report furnished to Central Force in numbers of S. Lindines. Weapons sent to II Army Camp depot Tunbridge Wells	} K.T.R.
	Report called for by Central Zone as to Nos of Japanese rifles and continue still in possession of Division	K.T.R
7.12.15. "	Saw OC Ordnance of SO, on various matters	K.T.R
8.12.15. "	Reports Central Zone re condition of .303 arms received	} K.T.R
	Reports to Third Army as to 90 mm Guns in possession	
9.12.15. "	Reports Central Zone through Third Army Nos of Italy rifles + carbines still in possession	K.T.R

Army Form C. 2118.

DADOS
61ST (S.M.) Division

WAR DIARY
INTELLIGENCE SUMMARY

(Erase heading not required.)

Instructions regarding War Diaries and Intelligence Summaries are contained in F. S. Regs., Part II. and the Staff Manual respectively. Title pages will be prepared in manuscript.

Hour, Date, Place	Summary of Events and Information	Remarks and references to Appendices
10.12.15 Boreham	NIL	
11.12.15 "	Reports Third Army receipt of 3600 nds Shrapnel Shell	K&R
12.12.15 "	NIL	K&R
13.12.15 "	Returns rendered as follows :-	
	(1) Canvas S&U in possession of Division — Third Army	
	(2) Nos. of dummy cartridges & clips available for transfer — "	
	(3) 18 pr equipment received to date — { Third Army / Central Force }	K&R
	(4) Breech [Knap] 5" Bl. Howitzer — { Third Army / 10th M. Central Force }	
14.12.15 "	Received intimation that a small no. of antigas helmets are being issued to the Division. Obtained distribution list from 4/50	K&R
15.12.15 "	Reported that all 18/pr equipment now received { Third Army / Central Force }	K&R
16.12.15 "	G.S. limbered wagons arriving for Infantry. Extended conference 10 am.	K&R
17.12.15 "	Reported on storage of Artillery Ammn to Third Army	K&R
	" no Surges to Third Army	K&R
18.12.15 "	NIL	
19.12.15 "		K&R

1247 W 3299 200,000 (E) 8/14 J.B.C. & A. Forms/C. 2118/12.

WAR DIARY / INTELLIGENCE SUMMARY

Army Form C. 2118

DADOS.
61st (S.M.) Division

Place	Date	Hour	Summary of Events and Information	Remarks and references to Appendices
Burham	20/12/15		Received telephone information from Central Force that the 109 Wagons G.S. released by issue of Infantry wagons to Infantry units, may be retained by Divisional Train, to serve their requirements. Interviewed by Major Gen Bannatine-Allason, when he requested information regards my state of equipment of the Division re. Range finders (b) Issue of Infantry units	KDR
"	21/12/15		All sandbags for general purposes now issued	KDR KDR
"	22/12/15		NIL. Went on leave until 24/12/15, Lieut Wethford acting in my absence	
"	23/12/15		Returns sent to Third Army as under:- (i) Equipment from all units transferred to 83rd Provisional Battn. (ii) Method of carrying blankets, Heavy Batteries (iii) Supply of Cable Electric for Artillery	K.P.W.
"	24/12/15		In response to Central Force telegram, wired Hd Qrs Central Force that 141 O.S. Wagons Mark X required to complete units to Authorised Establishment	K.P.W. K.P.W.
"	25/12/15		Dispatched duplicate copies of the Report on '303 in. Arms, which was forwarded to Central Force on 8/12/15	K.P.W.
"	26/12/15		NIL.	K.P.W.
"	27/12/15		Returned from leave. O/C Divisional Cyclist Coy reports receipt of the following:- 193 Rifles L.L.E. MKI*, 193 Sword bayonets P/88 MKIII, 193 Scabbards Sword bayonet, 58,100 rds SAA .303 MK VII in charge us. Report's receipt of same to Third Army.	KDR

WAR DIARY

INTELLIGENCE SUMMARY

Army Form C. 2118

DADOS 61st (S.M.) Division

(Erase heading not required.)

Instructions regarding War Diaries and Intelligence Summaries are contained in F.S. Regs, Part II and the Staff Manual respectively. Title Pages will be prepared in manuscript.

Place	Date	Hour	Summary of Events and Information	Remarks and references to Appendices
K.R. Graham	28/12/15	—	Received new hostly ckun Store Table for Howitzer Bde. Circulated same. Received list of civilian transport wagons required by Artillery. — Instructed O/C ASC. to supply same. New contract for worn out clothing received and circulated.	K.R.
"	29/12/15	—	Received notification from Woolwich that the 141 G.S. wagons required to complete the Division in this respect will be issued shortly.	K.R.
"	30/12/15	—	Wires Ordnance Officer Colchester re G.S. wagon Equipment.	K.R.
"	31/12/15	—	I.O.M. Central Force called re fitting Brackets to 5" Howitzers. — Instructed CRA at his request.	K.R.

In addition to the above the usual office routine work was proceeded with each day. — Equipment coming along fairly well, & substantial progress made.

K. Sangermaner Kent

Lt. A.O.D.
D.A.D. O.S. 61st DIV. T.F.

Confidential

War Diary

of

PATROS 61st DIVISION

from 1st January to 31st January 1916.

Army Form C. 2118

WAR DIARY
or
INTELLIGENCE SUMMARY
(Erase heading not required.)

DADOS.
61st Division

JAN. 1ST to JAN. 31ST 1916.

Place	Date	Hour	Summary of Events and Information	Remarks and references to Appendices
Boreham	1/1/16	—	NIL.	K.S.R.
"	2/1/16	—	NIL.	K.S.R.
"	3/1/16	—	NIL.	K.S.R.
"	4/1/16	—	Statement shewing Nos. of Unserviceable Impressed Vehicles in possession of Division sent to THIRD ARMY for instructions as to disposal	K.S.R.
			Telegram from THIRD ARMY enquiring No. of rounds Shrapnel shell actually in possession of Divisional Artillery. — REPLY:- 3600 rds 18/pr. Shrapnel shell, 4 rds of which in possession of 2/3 BRIGADE, marked "without explosives".	
"	5/1/16	—	Return sent to CENTRAL FORCE (copy to THIRD ARMY) shewing arms and ammunition in possession of all units of Division.	K.S.R.
"	6/1/16	—	THIRD ARMY reply re Impressed Vehicles that disposal of same is under consideration by WAR OFFICE.	K.S.R.
"	7/1/16	—	Reported to THIRD ARMY that stores for four 90 mm guns not yet received.	K.S.R.
			" " " " re Dial Sights and Adapters for Howitzer Brigade, shewing No. required.	
			Reported to THIRD ARMY regarding release of 90 mm equipment, stating same cannot take place until receipt of adapters for Dial Sights	K.S.R.

Army Form C. 2118

WAR DIARY
INTELLIGENCE SUMMARY
(Erase heading not required.)

PAROS
61st. Division

JAN. 1st to JAN. 31st 1916.

Place	Date	Hour	Summary of Events and Information	Remarks and references to Appendices
Boreham	4/1/16	—	Applied THIRD ARMY for permission to purchase Hand Grenade Castings from the BENGAL FOUNDRY COY	K&R.
"	"	—	Application by CRA to return 10 unserviceable magazines for cordering 18 pr. equipment forwarded to THIRD ARMY	
"	"	—	Application by 183rd INFY. BDE for issue of a Second Drummy Machine Gun forwarded THIRD ARMY.	
"	"	—	Reported to D.D.O.S. WOOLWICH through THIRD ARMY N° of DIAL SIGHTS N°1 required to complete 90 mm. guns, and raised point as to ditto for 18 pr	
"	6/1/16	—	Reported THIRD ARMY position as regards release of 90 mm. equipment, attaching Report of CRA.	K&R.
"	"	"	Obtained issue for Jan 10. of Blank S.A.A. .303, 2000 rds to YEOMANRY, 100 to DIVISIONAL CYCLIST COMPANY — Covering approval requested by C.O. COLCHESTER for latter Issue. Applied THIRD ARMY for same.	
"	"	"	Detailed LIEUT. WEBB, ADR. to attend Clothing Board at Colchester, on instructions received from ADOS THIRD ARMY.	
"	9/1/16	"	92 sets harness issued to Hqr. Coy. ASC. Periscopes issued, two to each INFANTRY UNIT, except 2/6 & 2/7 WARWICK REGTS.	K&R.
"	10/1/16	"	NIL	K&R.
"	11/1/16	"	Received reply from THIRD ARMY on release of 90 mm. equipment. Forwarded THIRD ARMY + CO.O. COLC? weight of old horse shoes available for transfer. Received information that PISTOLS & BINOCULARS can now be issued to officers of this Division. Notified all formations and called for indents.	K&R.

Army Form C. 2118

(3)

WAR DIARY
—or—
INTELLIGENCE SUMMARY
(Erase heading not required.)

DANOS
61st. DIVISION

JAN 1st to JAN 31st 1916.

Instructions regarding War Diaries and Intelligence Summaries are contained in F. S. Regs., Part II. and the Staff Manual respectively. Title Pages will be prepared in manuscript.

Place	Date	Hour	Summary of Events and Information	Remarks and references to Appendices
Boreham	12/1/16	—	Forwarded to THIRD ARMY in bulk Certificates re monthly Clothing Boards	K&R
"	"	—	" " Nos. of Rds. KYNOCK Cartridges .22 in possession	
"	"	—	Visited C.R.E. re BOARDS OF SURVEY on Clothing & Equipment.	
"	13/1/16	—	Reported THIRD ARMY that 4 Machine Horse Clothing on loan to 2/1 SM.BDE. R.F.A. have been returned to THIRD ARMY CAMP DEPOT today	K&R
"	"	—	Visited C.R.A. re BOARDS OF SURVEY on Clothing & Equipment	
"	"	—	Periscopes No.19 — Two issued to 2/1 GLOS BTY.	
"	14/1/16	—	Reported THIRD ARMY position as regards rendition of Camp Accounts	K&R
"	"	—	Received notification from WOOLWICH that Sufficient G.S. WAGONS to complete DIVISION are now under issue	
"	15/1/16	—	Periscopes No.II. Two issued to SIGNAL COY, & two to 2/6 R.WARWICK REGT.	K&R
"	16/1/16	—	NIL.	K&R
"	17/1/16	—	THIRD ARMY asked re procuring rifles to bring up to strength of 850	K&R
"	18/1/16	—	Received notification from CENTRAL FORCE that unserviceable Mule Harness may be sold locally. Referred matter to C.O.O. COLCHESTER.	K&R

1875 Wt. W593/826 1,000,000 4/15 J.B.C. & A. A.D.S.S./Forms/C. 2118.

Army Form C. 2118

WAR DIARY or INTELLIGENCE SUMMARY

(Erase heading not required.)

Instructions regarding War Diaries and Intelligence Summaries are contained in F.S. Regs., Part II. and the Staff Manual respectively. Title Pages will be prepared in manuscript.

JAN 1st to JAN 31st 1916.

DEPOT 61st DIVISION

Place	Date	Hour	Summary of Events and Information	Remarks and references to Appendices
Boreham	19/1/16	—	Circulated G.O.C's instructions for redistribution of '22 Rifles. Despatched to THIRD ARMY. Proceeding aboard Survey on Clothing Equipment Received notification from THIRD ARMY that Gravity Firewood fighting material may be drawn by the Division from the School at KELVEDON — Passes to C.R.E. as instructed by G.S.	} K&R
	20/1/16		Received notification from WEEDON that 100 short rifles per Inf. Bn. under issue. Informed Inf. Genls./Staff THIRD ARMY, G.S. 61st DIVISION & INFY. BDES.	} K&R
	21/1/16 22/1/16		Received instructions from THIRD ARMY for handing of Japanese Arms & Amm" to Provender Brigades	
	23/1/16		Trench fighting Stores at KELVEDON. Amusement received from THIRD ARMY NIL.	} K&R
	24/1/16		WIRED CENTRAL FORCE (copy THIRD ARMY) re number of wagons for 1st AMM COLS, position not being clear on latest tables. Forwarded THIRD ARMY return of Kentage in possession	} K&R
			THIRD ARMY require notification when each INFY UNIT receives 100 Short Rifles	
	25/1/16		THIRD ARMY information re provision of Vehicle Lamps received	} K&R
	"		" " " " that no gun boots will be issued	
	"		Forwarded Ry School – THIRD ARMY ask requirements; passed to Q Reported to THIRD ARMY that 5" Bl. Howitzer Way out Limber Brakes are O.P.	

Army Form C. 2118

WAR DIARY
—or—
INTELLIGENCE SUMMARY
(Erase heading not required.)

DADOS 61st DIVISION

JAN 1st to JAN 31st 1916

Instructions regarding War Diaries and Intelligence Summaries are contained in F.S. Regs., Part II. and the Staff Manual respectively. Title Pages will be prepared in manuscript.

Place	Date	Hour	Summary of Events and Information	Remarks and references to Appendices
Brixham	26/1/16	—	33 Bicycles issued to 1/3 3rd Coy SWRE.	} WAR
"	"	3 PM	By Genl's orders inspected ledgers & equipment deficiencies of No 3 Coy ASC.	
"	27/1/16	—	33 Bicycles issued to 2/7 3rd Coy SWRE	} WAR
"	"	2.30 PM	Attended meeting with AADQMG at HQRS 2/8 R. WAR. REGT, enquiring into deficiencies on wagons of 2/5, 2/7 & 2/8 R. WAR. REGTS. Reported late to AADQMG 16 Prismatic Binoculars & 2 Telescopes to be issued to each INFY. BN. at an early date.	} WAR
"	28/1/16	—	Received notification from THIRD ARMY that 15/in guns will shortly be substituted for 2/4 HOW. BDE.	} KAR
"	"	"	Report received from CRA forwarded to THIRD ARMY re release of 90 mm guns.	KAR
"	29/1/16	"	Applies 10 M.C.T. for History sheets of 18/in guns recently received. THIRD ARMY enquire re defective of Artillery Signalling Equipment. Replies that COLCHESTER has been hastened for reply.	} KAR
"	30/1/16	"	NIL.	
"	31/1/16	"	CRA intimates that 4 5"BL Howitzer guns & wagons are to be received shortly from HAVRE — Informed THIRD ARMY & received instructions.	} WAR

K. Sangkunevan
Lt. A.O.D.
D.A.D.O.S. 61st DIV.

Army Form C. 2118.

WAR DIARY
or
INTELLIGENCE SUMMARY.
(Erase heading not required.)

May 1916

DADOS
61. DIVN

Instructions regarding War Diaries and Intelligence Summaries are contained in F. S. Regs., Part II. and the Staff Manual respectively. Title pages will be prepared in manuscript.

Place	Date	Hour	Summary of Events and Information	Remarks and references to Appendices
In the Field	14/5/16	12.40	Arrived BOULOGNE with second Advance Party of Division. Reported to Base Commandant.	X/R
	18/5/16	9.0	Proceeded by car, to GHQ, Hqrs XI Army Corps, & arrived destination ST. VENANT.	X/R
	19/5/16	—	Proceeded with Staff to Estaires round Billeting areas of Division.	X/R
	20/5/16	—	Visited ADOS XI Corps & with him DADOS 39th Division to see system adopted	X/R
	21/5/16	—	Arranged site for Divisional Ordnance Dump, & used Base for 2 Store Tents for same. Visited ADOS XI Corps, also Field Cashier XI Corps, & opened Imprest Account.	
	22/5/16	—	Visited DADOS 35th Division to see system adopted.	X/R
	23/5/16	—	Visited DADOS 38th Division — ditto —	X/R
	24/5/16	—	Visited DADOS 35th Division & arranged that on arrival my Warrant Officers should spend a day with his Warrant Officers to learn system.	X/R
	25/5/16	—	Hqrs Division arrived. Visited DADOS 1st Army.	X/R
	26/5/16	—	Warrant Officers arrived. Visited DADOS 35th Division.	X/R
	27/5/16 to 31/5/16	—	System inaugurated and instructions issued through Divisional Routine Orders as to Ordnance Service in the Field.	X/R

A Hughson Roberts Capt.
D. A. D. O. S. 61st DIV.

Confidential

WAR DIARY

JUNE 1916.

RA DDS 61st DIVISION B.E.F.

Army Form C. 2118.

WAR DIARY
or
INTELLIGENCE SUMMARY.
(Erase heading not required.)

DADOS
61. DIV

June 1916

Place	Date	Hour	Summary of Events and Information	Remarks and references to Appendices
ST VENANT	1/6/16	—	Recd. Divisional Reserve 20,000 Goodrich's PH – Obtained from DO 11 Corps reqts. 900 steel helmets & issued same to Bdns. in trenches.	KtR
"	4/6/16	—	Recd. Cutters Wire SAA for Divn; On Corps instructions demanded 21 Stokes guns to complete Divn. —	KtR
"	5/6/16	—	Order Communications Stoppages issue of 21 Stokes Guns	KtR
"	6/6/16	—	3000 Steel helmets recd.	KtR
"	7/6/16	—	6345 " "	KtR
"	8/6/16	—	9 Stokes Guns recd from OD XI Corps.	KtR
"	9/6/16	—	1906 Steel helmets recd.	KtR
"	10/6/16	—	On being informed that 61 Div would relieve 36 Div shortly, went to LA GORGUE to arrange taking over Ordnance Dump & Office. Informed ADOS XI Corps & asked as regards demands for & supply of special stores authorised by G.R.O.s &c.	KtR
"	11th		DADOS 36th Divn came to arrange taking over of Ordnance Dump at ST VENANT. Loaded up lorries with Stores & officer effects.	KtR
"	12th		Removed office & to site that recently occupied by DADOS 36 Divn at LA GORGUE. Cleared Rifflehead – Position normal by 3.P.M	KtR

Army Form C. 2118.

WAR DIARY
INTELLIGENCE SUMMARY: DADOS
51 DIV.
(Erase heading not required.)

Place	Date	Hour	Summary of Events and Information	Remarks and references to Appendices
LA GORGUE	13/6		Obtained two No 14 periscopes. Handed to GRA	KAR
	14/6		Rec'd 12 2-inch Trench Mortars for Medium TM Batteries	KAR
			Obtained 193 periscopes various from 36 Div for use of troops in Trenches.	KAR
	15/6		Rec'd 12 Vickers Guns complete. Issued to 1st & 3rd INF BDE	KAR
	16/6		Rec'd 20 " " " " Issue suspended by DHQ	KAR
	17/6		Rec'd 21 Stokes 3" guns, 25 No 14 Periscopes, 156 MG Periscopes – 100 Bombers helmets	KAR
			100 Impulline Mills fuse, 36 rifle grenades	
	18/6		Ordered 2 rifle batteries, 2 pivot mounts for Vickers gun from Heavy Mobile Workshop	KAR
	19/6		3 Machine gun Companies arrived from Home Forces DIVN, complete with guns	KAR
			Requested CRE's instructions re disposal of 32 Vickers guns.	KAR
	20/6		Obtained conference with ADOS XI Corps and all DADOS's of Corps re plan of	KAR
	22/6		action for Ordnance Services in event of move forward	KAR
	25/6		Rec'd 24 3.9" Trench mortars for Stokes purposes. Issued as directed	KAR
	26/6		Consigned 32 Vickers guns to Base.	KAR
			Rec'd one No 24 (experimental) Periscope	KAR

Army Form C. 2118.

WAR DIARY
~~INTELLIGENCE~~ SUMMARY.
(Erase heading not required)

ADOS 61 DIV

Place	Date	Hour	Summary of Events and Information	Remarks and references to Appendices
LA GORGUE	28/6	—	Informed in writing that each INF BN to receive 2 more Lewis Guns. Wires Base for same	WR
	29/6	—	2/5 Warwicks short 2 Lewis Guns not yet taken — Wires Base for 2 to replace	WR
	30/6	—	States DIV ARMOURERS SHOP with 3 armourers withdrawn, 1 from each INF BDE	WR

Special Remarks:—
Spare parts Lewis Guns exceedingly difficult to obtain.

K. Fanshaw Roberts Capt

[Stamp: D.A.D.O.S. 5 JUL 1916 61ST DIVISION]

Army Form C. 2118.

WAR DIARY
INTELLIGENCE SUMMARY.
(Erase heading not required.)

DADOS 61st DIVN

July 1916

Instructions regarding War Diaries and Intelligence Summaries are contained in F. S. Regs., Part II. and the Staff Manual respectively. Title pages will be prepared in manuscript.

Place	Date	Hour	Summary of Events and Information	Remarks and references to Appendices
LABORGUE	2/4/16	—	Received 2 Lewis Guns for 2/5 Warwicks to replace unserviceable. Calls for report on 8 staff of Lewis Guns in Divn. Base Wires "Lewis Gun spare parts not available"	KWR
"	3/7		Demanded 3 Lewis Guns to replace unserviceable through lack of spares Received 8 telemeters with Raswin bubbles for Artillery	KWR
"	5/7		Received 24 Lewis Guns & sufficient to provide 2 more to each Inf. Bn (making six now held by each Bn) & 3 to replace Unserviceable, demanded on 2/7/16	KWR
"	6/7		Received 16 pr experimental wire [frog?] gloves.	KWR
"	4/7		One Pewforming extruder to be [Built?]	KWR
"	8/7		DADOS I Army calls re system ; with him on MAQMG.	KWR
"	12/7		Visits 154 Inf Bde at Richebourg St Vaast	KWR
"	13/7		"Gumboothan mourning"	KWR
"	15/7		8th Divl Art. arrives. Demanded buffers and horseshoes for them	KWR
"	16-20/7		Division in action. Demanded 9 Vickers & 10 Lewis Guns to replace losses	KWR
"	20/7		Demanded 3 more Vickers & 2 more Lewis Guns to replace destroyed	KWR
"	23/7		Sent DDOS I Army full explanation re Lewis & McKean Guns.	KWR

Army Form C. 2118.

Continued
Page 2
July 1916

WAR DIARY
or
INTELLIGENCE SUMMARY.

PARCC
61 DIV.

(Erase heading not required.)

Instructions regarding War Diaries and Intelligence Summaries are contained in F. S. Regs., Part II. and the Staff Manual respectively. Title pages will be prepared in manuscript.

Place	Date	Hour	Summary of Events and Information	Remarks and references to Appendices
La Gorgue	25/7	–	Returned 5 Lewis guns to Base, not now required, as the number previously reported had now arrived.	K+R.
	26/7	–	Serious shortage of springs. Running out for 18 pr. Reported to II Corps – Shortage at Base.	K+R
	27/7	–	Shortage of Latch Springs for Lewis gun magazines – New pattern latch spring very inferior to old Pattern. Shortage of spare parts for Vickers Guns. Special point : Shortage of Springs Running Out. Lewis, Vickers, 18/pr QF Lewis Gun spare part. Vickers Gun .303 spare part. Lewis gun new magazine Latch Springs.	K+R

H.a phaembrent
PARCC 61 DIV. Corps

BEF
2/8/16

T2134. Wt. W703—776. 500000. 4/15. Sir J. C. & S.

Army Form C. 2118.

WAR DIARY
DADOS 61st DIVN
INTELLIGENCE SUMMARY. AUGUST. 1916.
B.E.F.

(Erase heading not required.)

Instructions regarding War Diaries and Intelligence Summaries are contained in F. S. Regs., Part II. and the Staff Manual respectively. Title pages will be prepared in manuscript.

Place	Date	Hour	Summary of Events and Information	Remarks and references to Appendices
LA GORGUE	AUG 1916 2nd		1 Army Heavy Mobile Workshop reported work held up owing to lack of SPRINGS Running Out QF 13 18/r. Hastened Base	K+R
"	3rd		Base Reports none available at present	
"	9th		Two Vickers Guns lost by shell fire, 162 BDE. M.G. Coy. Wires Base for two	K+R
"	10th		Wires Base for Steel Helmets requires for draft arriving from day to day	K+R
"	11th		Sergt. Soler posted as Brigade Warrant Officer to 63 Division	K+R
"			Two Vickers Guns received for 162 BDE. M.G. Coy.	K+R
"	12th		Experimental Steel Necklet for Bombers received & issued	K+R
"	15th		A.I.A inspects Armourers Shop &c.	K+R
"	20th		Heavy French Mortar Bty found - Demands Stores for same	K+R
"	27th		Springs R.O. QZ 13 018/r received for 1 Army Heavy Mobile W'shop.	K+R
"			Six French pattern Signalling Lamps received & issued	K+R
"	28		Enlarged Divisional Armourers Shop to 4 armourers	K+R
"			Special Note:- Lewis Gun Spare Parts Still slow in arriving, we are Waiting wiring to Base when Guns out of action	

N. Vaughman Breet Capt.
DADOS. 61st DIVN

31 AOU 1916

WAR DIARY

Vol 5

D.A.D.O.S. 61st. DIVISION. B.E.F.

September 1916.

Vol. 5.

WAR DIARY

INTELLIGENCE SUMMARY

VOL. I
PAROS. 61st DIVN.
BEF
Sept 1-30 1916.

Army Form C. 2118.

Place	Date	Hour	Summary of Events and Information	Remarks and references to Appendices
LA GORGUE.	1/9/16	—	Authority received to complete each Battn. with 8 Lewis Guns. Demanded 26 from Base. Wired Base for one 3" TRENCH MORTAR for 184 T.M.BTY to replace one destroyed.	K+R
"	3/9/16	—	Received 26 LEWIS GUNS and one 3" MORTAR as demanded on 1st inst.	K+R
"	4/9/16	—	Visited 10M T Army Heavy Mobile Workshop with Divl Trench Mortar Officer re cause of feed mechanisms blowing out so frequently.	K+R
"	5/9/16	—	Inspected VICKERS GUNS of 184 B.M.G. Coy.	K+R
"	6/9/16	—	C.R.O. 516 states all unserviceable S.D. Clothing to be returned to me, not Batth. Initiated scheme accordingly; reception of such clothing every Wednesday, 10 Shoulder horns received, without connections.	K+R
"	8/9/16	—	Received 100,000 Sandbags for use as beds on scale of 6 per man.	K+R
"	10/9/16	—	Received 4,000 prs. Gum Boots Thigh.	K+R
"	12/9/16	—	Received 1080 F.S. Boots for 25% wounded men of Division	K+R
"	13/9/16	—	Wired Base for one 18 PR and Carriage for B/306 BB, to replace totally unserviceable	K+R
"	15/9/16	—	Received " " " Division completed with STEEL HELMETS.	K+R

WAR DIARY

DADOS 61 DIVN
SEPT. 1916

Page 2.

Army Form C. 2118.

INTELLIGENCE SUMMARY.

Place	Date	Hour	Summary of Events and Information	Remarks and references to Appendices
LA GORGUE	16/9/16	—	Divl. Arty. reorganised as 6 Gun 18 pr Btys, How Btys remaining 4 Gun: 305 Bde and C/308 therefore disbanded - Took necessary action with Base, and informed units to return surplus stores to me	K+R
"	20/9/16	—	42 LEWIS GUN HANDCARTS received. Demanded one 3" MORTAR for 183 TM Bty to replace destroyer	K+R
"	23/9/16	—	Received "	K+R
"	25/9/16	—	Received further 1850 GUM BOOTS THIGH, none yet issued to units pending DHQ instructions	K+R
"	26/9/16	—	Returned all surplus RA stores due to reorganization	K+R
"	29/9/16	—	Ordnance Dump & Armourers Shop inspected by:- DADOS I Army, A.MQMG XI Corps AA QMG 61st DIVN. Two Russian Officers and various stores explained to latter Connections for STROMBOS HORNS received, of wrong size	K+R

Special Note:- Better supplies of LEWIS GUN PARTS received during month.
Experimental elevating & traversing stand (weighing 3 lbs) made in DIVL
Armourers Shop & very favourably reported on by Infantry Bdes.

K. Toughsanson R Beck
Capt.

VOL. 6   Oct. 1

Army Form C. 2118.

WAR DIARY
or
INTELLIGENCE SUMMARY.
(Erase heading not required.)

DADOS
61. DIV

Instructions regarding War Diaries and Intelligence Summaries are contained in F.S. Regs., Part II. and the Staff Manual respectively. Title pages will be prepared in manuscript.

Place	Date	Hour	Summary of Events and Information	Remarks and references to Appendices
LA GORGUE	6/10/16	—	16 Trestle mountings for Lewis Guns Received. One Vickers Gun demanded for 183 Bde M.G. Coy to replace "U".	K&R
"	7/10/16	—	12 Lewis gun Haversacks received. Received Vickers Gun for 183 B.M.G. Coy.	K&R
"	8/10/16	—	Tear Horn received from base with wrong chaplet called in & fitted in Armourers shop. Reserve of R.H. Helmets reduced to 5000.	K&R
"	9/10/16	—	Demanded one 2" Mortar for 3. 61 B/y K.R. reflame destroyed.	K&R
"	10/10/16	—	Received same	K&R
"	11/10/16	—	10 Tear Helmets received.	K&R
"	12/10/16	—	Leather Jerkins for Infy & Box Respirators received.	K&R
"	15/10/16	—	Received notice Division moving shortly.	K&R
"	19/10/16	—	Suspenses payment names from Calais.	K&R
"	22/"	—	Wire ADOS 1st Corps giving my arrangements for move, suspensions of indents etc.	K&R
"	23/"	—	DADOS 56 DIVN arrived; arranged date for handing over, & ask to transfer of attached troops & Divl. Artillery.	K&R
"	24/"	—		K&R

T2134. Wt. W708—776. 500000. 4/15. Sir J. C. & S.

WAR DIARY
or
INTELLIGENCE SUMMARY.
(Erase heading not required.)

Army Form C. 2118.

OCT. Page II

Place	Date	Hour	Summary of Events and Information	Remarks and references to Appendices
LAGORGUE	Oct. 25	—	Arranged temporary dump for DADOS 56 DIVN.	WR
"	26	—	Received full complement horses rugs greatcoats &c.	WR
"	28	—	DIVN marched to ST VENANT area, except RA & No 1 Coy ASC	WR
"	29	—	Loaded up 2 trucks on rail with stores for destination DADOS I Army Cellar	WR
"	30	—	Left LAGORGUE and arrived ST VENANT	WR
"	31	—	Arranged reception & despatch of all unserviceable clothing.	WR

N. Humphreys Roberts
Capt ADOS

DADOS 61 DIVN.
9/11/19

WAR DIARY.

51st DIVN.
Nov 1 – 30 1916.

Vol. VII

WAR DIARY
or
INTELLIGENCE SUMMARY.

Army Form C. 2118.

RA 2OS. 61ST DIVN.
Nov. 1 – 30 1916.

Place	Date	Hour	Summary of Events and Information	Remarks and references to Appendices
ST VENANT	Nov. 1	–	Went to BRUAY – recony: trucks – Saw ADOS XI Corps. Suspense all comes from CAZINS. Ready. Definite instructions re move.	KAK
"	2	–	Wired to CHELERS	KAK
CHELERS	3	–	Saw BDES. III Army. Ascertain Railhead to 61 would be FREVENT	KAK
"	4	–	Wires CAZINS for several stores to arrive Tt.	KAK
"	5	–	Went to ROELLECOURT arranges Dump	KAK
ROELLECOURT	6	–	Went to FROHEN LE GRAND to arrange Billets	KAK
"	6	–	Moved to "	KAK
F. LE GRAND	–	–	Trouble with Lewis gun dead wheels – Round tyres useless –	KAK
"	7	–	Received heaps of Inf: of that. Very uniform quality – further supplies about received – Informed BDES III Army + more BDES III Army instruct Bases as to transferring wheels.	KAK
"	8	–	Went FREVENT Saw Rev. Nurse 162, 163, 184 INF BDES	KAK
"	9	–	Obtained return showing numbers of Lewis Guns/out carts with Round tyres wheels in possession, 1st 40 army 116 flat	KAK
"	10	–	Wrote HMRE demanding exchanges for flat tyres wheels. Wrote to Railhead and ROULLENS	KAK

Army Form C. 2118.

WAR DIARY
—of—
INTELLIGENCE SUMMARY.
(Erase heading not required.)

RA 900 61 DIV
Nov 1–30 — Page 2.

Place	Date	Hour	Summary of Events and Information	Remarks and references to Appendices
	Nov			
FROHEN LE GRAND	11	—	New Railhead BOUQUEMAISON. Chaussée mule train at FIENVILLERS Ral head. Large consignment huts received, instructions from Reserve Army head qtrs to complete DMR.	WAR
"	12–14	—	Inspected units of Division	WAR
"	15	—	Moves to BERNAVILLE	WAR
BERNAVILLE	16	—	" " CANAPLES	WAR
CANAPLES	17	—	" " CONTAY	WAR
CONTAY	18	—	Saw RA 2nd Corps — arranged Dump	WAR
"	19	—	Local purchases at AMIENS	WAR
"	20	—	Pits selected ALBERT & BOUZINCOURT to arrange Dumps	WAR
"	22	—	Moved to BOUZINCOURT	WAR
BOUZINCOURT	23	—	Reconnaissance of the heavy Supposed arrayed mm Dump	WAR
"	24	—	Practise from Railway AVELUY — Took over stores from 18 DIVN at ALBERT —	WAR
"	26	—	RA 900 ST DIVN arrived & took my site of DUMP. Moved mine to HEDAUVILLE 1gk DIVN Arty attached to me	WAR

WAR DIARY

INTELLIGENCE SUMMARY — Nov. 1-30 P. 3

Place	Date	Hour	Summary of Events and Information	Remarks
HEDAU-VILLE	Nov 23	—	Stove burning wood nets — Ordnance param thefts — killed 49. Some stores damaged.	
"	26		Makes new building, received renewed 15 tons stores	

General Note on Roer Truck of Nov 50 miles:—

(1) Salves, more or less (Ordnance system when broken works) without notice of Railheads are not arranged for sufficient for sheep. Roads not of stores being ordered up — The troops suffer from want of Boots especially.

(2) Refaries trots (at BKSE) are useless for marching any distance.

(3) Lorries [guard] ambulances are not sufficiently well designed for travelling over rough roads.

(4) Suggest there should be small Ordnance Supply Depôts in each areas [with] sufficient stores & staff, that passing through, as transport permits, our packed spares being continuous supply. current No⁸

3/12/16. K Cunynchame Roberts Capt AVS
D.ADVS. 61st Div N.

WAR DIARY.

D.A.D.O.S. 61st DIVISION.
B.E.F.

DECEMBER 1916.

VOL. 8.

WAR DIARY ~~INTELLIGENCE SUMMARY~~

(Erase heading not required.)

DADOS. 61st DIVN. B.E.F.
DEC. 1916.

Vol 8

Army Form C. 2118.

Instructions regarding War Diaries and Intelligence Summaries are contained in F.S. Regs., Part II. and the Staff Manual respectively. Title pages will be prepared in manuscript.

Place	Date	Hour	Summary of Events and Information	Remarks and references to Appendices
HEDAUVILLE	1916 DEC. 3	—	Two more LEWIS GUNS for BATTN. (except PIONEERS) authorised (1 Estabt. now 10 per unit)	K&R
	4	—	Demanded same from BASE. Local purchases in AMIENS.	K&R
	5	—	LEATHER JERKINS 2,340 recd. completing INFANTRY. F.S. BOOTS, received sufficient to equip mounted men of Division.	
			Demanded one 4.5 HOW. & carriage for C/306 to replace V. (burst)	K&R
			one VICKERS GUN for 154 MGC to replace destroyed	K&R
	6		Received 20 tons BOOTS &c to complete DIVISION. ~~Withdrew 18 per to complete 153 MGC~~ K&R	K&R
	7		Received 24 LEWIS GUNS to complete each of 12 BNs to 10.	K&R
	8		" VICKERS GUN for 164 MGC.	K&R
	9		" 4.5 HOW. for C/306	K&R
	10		" 1000 undershirts fur to complete DIVN	K&R
	11		" Dupl. allotment of 60 SOYERS STOVES	K&R
	13.		" VICKERS GUN for 163 MGC. (delayed) Demanded 18 per for A/306 to replace scores	K&R K&R

Army Form C. 2118.

WAR DIARY

INTELLIGENCE SUMMARY

DADOS 61 DIV.
BEF December 1916
P. 2.

(Erase heading not required.)

Instructions regarding War Diaries and Intelligence Summaries are contained in F. S. Regs., Part II. and the Staff Manual respectively. Title pages will be prepared in manuscript.

Place	Date	Hour	Summary of Events and Information	Remarks and references to Appendices
HEDAUVILLE	1916 DEC. 13		Received 15,000 sets underclothing for DIVL BATHS	WAR
	14		Visited 10M No. 9 Ordce WORKSHOP LIGHT	WAR
	15		Local purchasing in AMIENS	WAR
	16		Recd. 100 sets Tent bottoms	WAR
	17		Recd. sufficient BOX RESPIRATORS small to complete DIVN & reserve	WAR
	20		" 2 GS Wagons for DIVL TRAIN to replace Destroyers	WAR
	21		Recd 80 Bombers Shields & Necklets for DIVN.	WAR
	22		Brought to notice of DHQ bad condition due to neglect of bicycles brought in for repair – got BRO mounted stating charge would be made for this.	WAR
			Two Field Cos & Pioneer Bn joined from 63 RN DIVN.	WAR
	23		Informed that another DIVL ARTILLERY coming shortly with ABOS Walking horses for Tents.	WAR
	25		Sent L.G. Stand as made in DIVL ARMOURERS SHOP to IV Corps L.G. School ST RIQUIER for trial.	WAR
	—		During month general routine work, Visiting Railhead, units, Salvage &c. Conferences at DHQ, also with ADOS IV Corps. Situation normal. Improved 13 Wir & Dump.	WAR

31 DEC 1916

A. Fanghman Roberts Capt
DADOS. 61st DIVN

WAR DIARY

HDQRS. 61st DIVN

VOL. IX

JANUARY 1917

Army Form C. 2118.

WAR DIARY
—or—
INTELLIGENCE SUMMARY.
(Erase heading not required.)

Instructions regarding War Diaries and Intelligence Summaries are contained in F.S. Regs., Part II. and the Staff Manual respectively. Title pages will be prepared in manuscript.

D.A.D.O.S.
61st DIVN.
1 FEB 1917

Place	Date	Hour	Summary of Events and Information	Remarks and references to Appendices
HEDAUVILLE	1917 JAN 1	—	Demanded 18ᵖʳ carriage, Dialsights & Telescope Sighting for A-307 RFA. 3 Lewis Guns for Instructional purposes.	K+R.
"	2	—	Received 15000 sets underclothing for DIVL BATHS.	K+R
"	3	—	Demanded 18ᵖʳ without carriage in BM. for A-306 RFA. Sent one SCOTT Lewis gun stand to GHQ school for trial.	K+R
"	4	—	Demanded 4.5 How: Complete for D-306 RFA to replace burst.	K+R
"	5	—	16ᵗʰ DIV. ARTY with WO, AOC & Lorry moved to me.	K+R
"	6	—	In view of impending move to back area by road hastened all wheels &c due. Saw ADOS IV CORPS & obtained approval of programme of move.	K+R
"	8	—	Received 1 Lewis gun for Instructional purposes. Cancelled other two due, as two received from GHQ. Wired DADsOS 16 & 2 n Divs that DADOS 51 Div & self will meet them tomorrow at BRAILLY, to arrange handing over.	K+R
"	9	—	Went to BUIGNY & BRAILLY with DADOS 51 DIV. Saw DADsOS 2ⁿᵈ & Chief of EUR & DADsOS 15 re handing over.	K+R
"	10	—	Sent by BRHS Mulvey warns, both of the Dun Lotaeches, to take place on 15th inst. to all concerned. Suspended payment advance Supreme Bases re new Railhead on 16th.	K+R

T2134. Wt. W708—776. 500000. 4/15. Sir J. C. & S.

Army Form C. 2118.

WAR DIARY
INTELLIGENCE SUMMARY.
(Erase heading not required.)

Instructions regarding War Diaries and Intelligence Summaries are contained in F. S. Regs., Part II. and the Staff Manual respectively. Title pages will be prepared in manuscript.

Page 2.

D.A.D.O.S.
61st DIVN.
1 FEB 1917

Place	Date	Hour	Summary of Events and Information	Remarks and references to Appendices
HEBUVILLE	1917 JAN 10	—	Demanded 16 p.t to replace 5 cast/ fm A-306-RFA.	K+R.
"	11	—	Wear car for HQ. 62 Bde RFA	K+R
"	12	—	Demanded 2400 Bayonets fighting sacks.	K+R
"	13	—	All leave given Lt T. M. Hantscene withdrawn & parties. Owing to shortage in supply of stationery ordered dry told received authority from	K+R
"	14	—	ADOS IV Corps to purchase up to £25. Removed suspension on any new Inserts. Took Stoll Ranges over to representative of DADOS 18th Div. (Base states no Bayonets fighting Sacks available — Asked authority to purchase. Demanded one 18 p.r fm C-307 with BM dramage	K+L
"	"	—	" " C-307 without " " To replace beyond local repair	K+L
"	"	—	" " 4.5 " fm C-306 with BM dramage	K+L
"	15	—	Moves from HEBUVILLE to BRAILLY, but left 1 WO, 1 OR & a lorry for Divn Artry r left behind with 16 Div.	K+L
BRAILLY	16	—	Erected shed for Divnl tools over Tents, Brazers r. & 146 leaves fm detachments from 2nd Divn.	K+L

Army Form C. 2118.

D.A.D.O.S.
61st DIVN.
1 FEB 1917

Page 3.

WAR DIARY
or
INTELLIGENCE SUMMARY.
(Erase heading not required.)

Instructions regarding War Diaries and Intelligence Summaries are contained in F. S. Regs., Part II. and the Staff Manual respectively. Title pages will be prepared in manuscript.

Place	Date	Hour	Summary of Events and Information	Remarks and references to Appendices
BEAUX.	1917 JAN. 18	-	Having received information that Divl Arty or N°1 Coy ASC start for the new area on 22nd. wrote to ADOS 18 DIV. to return my lorry & arrange a "move" three units on that date for me.	K+R
			Received 16/pr with 75M rearriage for C/307	
			18/pr gun ends for C/307	
			4.5 with 75M rearriage for C/308.	
	19	-	Saw ADOS II Corps at CRÉCY. Received first consignment of stores at BONNEVILLE. Ammunition arrived in new area. Received location list. Arranged refill unit at 4 dumps daily	K+R
	21	-	Received 24 Helmets & Box Respirators to complete Divl Reserve. Ascertained nearest Ordnance Workshop to be near CRÉCY - informed all units @ 1:45 each.	K+R
	23	-	Drawer 460 Saddles at FLIXECOURT.	K+R
	24	-	Saw OM of N°26 Workshop & arranged early inspection of guns & vehicles. 4.5 How. with 75M rearriage received for D/308.	K+R

Army Form C. 2118.

WAR DIARY
or
INTELLIGENCE SUMMARY.
(Erase heading not required.)

Instructions regarding War Diaries and Intelligence Summaries are contained in F. S. Regs., Part II. and the Staff Manual respectively. Title pages will be prepared in manuscript.

D.A.D.O.S. 61st DIVN. Page 4.
1 FEB 1917

Place	Date	Hour	Summary of Events and Information	Remarks and references to Appendices
BRAY	1917 JAN. 25	—	No trucks arrived. Local purchase in Ailleville of certain stores.	A+R
	26		No trucks arrived	A+R
	27		"	A+R
	28		"	
			Artillery rearrangement now effected. HQ, A,B,C Batteries 306 to leave Dunoon. D/306 & D/307 to be split up to complete D/306 & D/307 to six sun Batteries.	A+R
	29	—	Two trucks with SD clothing arrived at midnight, cleared by 3 am.	A+R
	30	—	No trucks. — Received notification that Dunoon moves on 4th prox.	A+R
	31	—	No trucks.	A+R
			Usual routine work, trust up work on large demands for paint etc for infantry weapons. Very little lighting possible in fact night available, especially in view of fact that no stores were received for a week.	

Kay... Roberts Col?
DADOS 61. DIV.

D.A.D.O.S. 61st DIVN.
1 FEB 1917

WAR DIARY.

D.A.D.O.S.
61st DIVN.
FEB. 1917.

WAR DIARY
Vol - X

Army Form C. 2118.

WAR DIARY DADOS. 61 DIV.
INTELLIGENCE SUMMARY. Feb. 1917.
(Erase heading not required.)

Instructions regarding War Diaries and Intelligence Summaries are contained in F. S. Regs., Part II. and the Staff Manual respectively. Title pages will be prepared in manuscript.

Place	Date	Hour	Summary of Events and Information	Remarks and references to Appendices
BRAMY	Feb 1917 1.	—	30 Tons arrived Railhead. 11 employees cleared & issued to troops.	AF&R
"	3	—	On IV Corps Instructions sent 30 Lewis Gun Handcarts to ABBEVILLE: Vehicles new area LONG. Selected Dump, Offices etc.	F+R
"	4	—	Sent balance of Lewis Gun Handcarts to ABBEVILLE (50)	F+R
"	5	—	Moved to LONG. Went Railhead — Reported arrived to IV Army. Engineers nearest	F+R
"	6	—	Order Workshop. Arranged & refilling points.	F+R
LONG	6	—	3 Lewis Cos, Pioneers, & R.W. Santerre Section reports Division	F+R
"	9	—	With 10M M.G. Order Depot Workshop inspection between 2/1 Warwicks also Mob. Vet. Sec. & Work T arranged repairs. Received warning order move 14th.	F+R
"	10	—	Moves for G.S. wagon for MG Coy etc.	F+R
"	13	—	Went to new area GUILLACOURT, arranged Dump etc.	F+R
"	14	—	Moved to GUILLACOURT. Arranged refilling points. Bad accommodation for stores, known nothing. Arranged as 2nd accommodation.	F+R
GUILLA-COURT	15	—	Large convoy new French Stove arrived. Cart refilling point 8 lorry loads.	F+R
"	16	—	6500 pro Gun Boots received & issued to R.W. Gun Boot Store.	F+R
"	17	—	Went to new area HARBONNIERES, arranged Dump, sent 6 lorry loads in.	F+R

Army Form C. 2118.

WAR DIARY DA/DS
G1 DIV (2)
INTELLIGENCE SUMMARY. FEB. 1917

(Erase heading not required.)

Place	Date	Hour	Summary of Events and Information	Remarks and references to Appendices
GUILLACOURT	Feb 1917 16	—	Moved to HARBONNIERES. Excellent accommodation arranged 2 refilling points for forward Brigades and one for Artillery. Other units to draw direct Reported position of 3 officer stores to 4th Army M.A. Corps.	ktR
HARBONNIERES	19	—	ADS IV Cullers inspected stores	ktR
"	20		Heavy consignment Trench stores. 56 Shrapnel horn regulators received but no communications. Wires Corps re same. Box Respirators & PH Helmet reserves completes	ktR
"	22		Issued Vermorel Sprayers Blankets for enquiries. Heavy demands for Gas appliances owing to enemy having large number Gasshells — able to meet all demands	ktR
"	24		endeavoured to reach 26 Workshop by car but roads impassable	ktR
"	25		Saw 10th 25 Workshop; arranged with him to undertake work, but Workshop appears to be a very great distance from Division; fully 12 miles.	ktR
"	26		GOC Division inspected Stores. Conversations re Shrapnel horn received answers	ktR

General Notice: Bad road conditions, but no shortage of stores. Roads restrictions relaxed in respect of Ordnance Stores. All French stores required for Division were taken over from Ahenine. Available from Base as rec.

Initials: Anthony Henson Robert Capt ADS

DA/DS. 61st Div

2 MAR 1917

T2134. Wt. W708-776. 500000. 4/15. Sir J. C. & S.

Vol XI

WAR DIARY.

MARCH 1917.

VOL. XI

DADOS. 61st DIVISION.

Army Form C. 2118.

Instructions regarding War Diaries and Intelligence
Summaries are contained in F. S. Regs., Part II.
and the Staff Manual respectively. Title pages
will be prepared in manuscript.

WAR DIARY
or
INTELLIGENCE SUMMARY.
(Erase heading not required.)

DADOS
61. DIV.
BEF.

March 1917
Page 1.

Place	Date	Hour	Summary of Events and Information	Remarks and references to Appendices
HARBONNIÈRES	1917 MAR. 1	—	3 Vickers Guns & 44 rifles issued to 163 Machine Gun Coy to replace lost in fire. Required 1500 pro sweep 9600 shirts for Divl Laundry.	K+R
"	2.		Went Railhead, also AMIENS and purchasing.	K+R
"	3		Received Divl Reserve 3000 Suits SD. — Opened new Clothing Store a Store for issue on payment to Officers with NCO in charge. Quantity Salvage French Rifles & SAA received — Arranged with French authorities to have same collected.	K+R
"	4		Owing to increasing Armourers work, divided Salvage to premises next door. Started BoK repairing Shop for Divisional Troops with 2 men from Poincum	K+R
"	5		Having ascertained by inspection that owing to bad condition of trenches or many rifles required stripping to clear mud or under side of barrel, made arrangements for work to be done in Divl. & Bde Armourers Shop. 3 Lewis guns received for 2/4 Oxfords to replace lost in action. Demanded 2 ditto for 2/5 GLOSTERS to replace "U".	K+R
"	6		Railhead changes from WIENCOURT to LA FLAQUE. Notes same	K+R K+R

Army Form C. 2118.

WAR DIARY
or
INTELLIGENCE SUMMARY.
(Erase heading not required.)

DADOS
61 DIV
BEF

March 1917
Page 2.

Place	Date	Hour	Summary of Events and Information	Remarks and references to Appendices
HARBONNIERES	1917 Mar 7.		Ammunr S/Sgt SCOTT went to IV Corps Schools for instruction in repair of instruments.	K+R
"	8.		Obtained 40 Rifle grenade stands & used 20 to bed INF BDE in the line.	K+R
"	17.		Went on leave to ENGLAND (10 days). Received warning order to	K+R
"	18.		Recalled from leave, owing to enemy retiring. Packed up office documents etc. Move at 2 hours notice. Received intimation that forward move would not take place for a few days.	K+R
"	19.		States office + staff again. Visited various Quartermasters & found all correct. Collected 100 sets Pack Saddlery 65 from OD IV Corps Troops, also 50 from 35 IN DIVN. Also Ammunition Carriers for Artillery. Issued same.	K+R
"	21		Took stock of all stores in hand & most necessary arrangements for handing over surplus to Salvage. Refilling of units suspenders, & was instructed to draw from Store. Went to LIHONS and CHAULNES (in ruins) to select site for stores in advent of being ordered to move there. Selected suitable spot to pitch store tent.	K+R

Army Form C. 2118.

WAR DIARY
or
INTELLIGENCE SUMMARY.
(Erase heading not required.)

DADJS.
61st DIV.
BEF.

March, 1917.
Page 3.

Place	Date	Hour	Summary of Events and Information	Remarks and references to Appendices
HARBONNIÈRES	1917 MAR 22	—	Collected 500 French Shelters from IV Corps Troops.	K+R.
"	23		282 A.T. Coy RE went for 20 Tents. Collected same from IV Corps & delivered them.	K+R.
			the units to IV Corps Troops. Drew 60 tents each for Canadian (Railway) Troops.	
"	25		Two additional sewing Guns per Battalion (except Pioneers) making 16 in all. Authority	K+R.
			War Base for same.	
"	26		Went to CROIX MOLIGNAUX to arrange site for Stores. Received intimation	K+R.
			that one wave forward on 29th. Wires Base not to send stores to arrive	
			28th or 29th inst.	
"	27		Despatched Rangers & Staffs & certain stores, in 4 lorries with instructions	K+R.
			to fold store tents & start erecting Shelters from material available.	
			Lorries returned, despatched them again with more stores & remainder of	
			personnel.	
"	28		Took Stock, handed certain stores to Salvage, left remainder in charge of	K+R.
			NCO & 1 man. I motored Office to CROIX MOLIGNAUX. Opened Office & store in	
"	29		large Nissen frame, mounted a guard at 5 pm	K+R.

Army Form C. 2118.

WAR DIARY
INTELLIGENCE SUMMARY.
(Erase heading not required.)

DADOS 61 DIV B.E.F.   March 1917   Page 4.

Place	Date	Hour	Summary of Events and Information	Remarks and references to Appendices
CROIX MOLIGNAUX	1917 MAR 30	—	Inspected roads round Stores, Craters at crossroads appeared dangerous & Murdered mine. All available men to reform lt. gramme work Bridle road from Inneo. RE's having reformed the other side only. Cleaned road to store of debris. Reached at MEZIERES, 35 miles borer, roads in terrible condition. Clearing of rubbish very difficult as ANZAC IV Corps cannot give me help with extra lorries. Lorries R–OR 56 has to complete journey each way. 1 broke down. Informed ANZAC IV Army ANZAC IV Corps positions of Stores Office. Completed Store Shelters for Brigade with 3 offices for self. Installed Chief Clerk in cellar. Erected Armourers & Bicycle & Shoemakers shops, also Lt. Othing Store.	K.R.
"	31	—	In afternoon all personnel worked on roads round Crater.	
		5 pm	Lorries returned having drawn one truck of Dumped contents of other at Railhead. Returned to Railhead 9 pm. Received 24 Lewis guns. Complex of each Battalion (except Pioneers) to 16.	K.R.

K Hauptmann Beet Col.

D.A.D.O.S.
61st DIVN.
31 MAR 1917

WAR DIARY

DIVISION. 61st DIVISION.

APRIL 1917.

VOL. 12.

Army Form C. 2118.

WAR DIARY
INTELLIGENCE SUMMARY.
(Erase heading not required.)

Diary 61st DIV" April 1917 Page 1.

Instructions regarding War Diaries and Intelligence Summaries are contained in F. S. Regs., Part II. and the Staff Manual respectively. Title pages will be prepared in manuscript.

Place	Date	Hour	Summary of Events and Information	Remarks and references to Appendices
CROIX MOLIGNAUX	April 1917 3.	—	Visits MONCHY LAGACHE with a view to finding a place nearer to line from which he troops could be refilled.	K+R
"	4	—	Owing to absence of Div BATHS took my party of unwashed & unshaved clothes-ridden & lousy troops to Divisional BATHS at GRUNICOURT to refill advanced troops.	K+R
"	5	—	Went to Railhead NESLE. Works ABDS & Corps & ArRes for next few days shelters.	T.U+R
"	6	—	Visits MONCHY LAGACHE with Chief Clerk, selected site for dump	K+R
"	8	12pm	Erected store-tent had our camp-site at MONCHY.	K+R
"	9	9pm	Received notification from BHQ "Divn am being relieved, stand fast"	K+R
"	10	—	Moves stores back from MONCHY	K+R
"	11	—	Received notification Division moving to Rest Area VOYENNES on 12th inst. Cleaves Railhead, 10 tons, Selected site for Camp at VOYENNES. Stores, Selectes refilling points.	K+R
"	12	—	Great part of stores there, 10 lorry loads small. 4 lorries from Supply Co. empty. Moves office to VOYENNES. Informs BDS & ARES. Arranges to continue to experience of BW PARTY although they were remaining in line with 35 DIVN	K+R

DADOS 61 DIV.
April 1917
Page 2

WAR DIARY
INTELLIGENCE SUMMARY
(Erase heading not required.)

Army Form C. 2118.

Place	Date	Hour	Summary of Events and Information	Remarks and references to Appendices
VOYENNES	1917 April 12		No 19 Ord Mob Workshop Lgt moves to the Dump at CROIX MOLIGNEAUX - Informed all units.	FfR
"	13		Owing to non-clearance of Brit. Salvage Officer, arranged Dump for reception of all Surplus & unserviceable Ordnance Stores.	FfR FfR
"	14		Attended Q Conference at DHQ - Transport Difficulties, French Shelters, Laundry, Refuse, Games, among Subjects discussed.	FfR
"	15		Ordnance reports from all Units on KITCHENS TRAVELLING, stoves 2g reg. pumps of an Coy, all Winch on TJM to unserviceable there Worth ADOS with suggestions for carrying rifle Grenades.	FfR FfR
"	16		Received information that the Divi Stands Nearly 32 m on 20 met -	FfR
"	17		Saw DADOS 32 DIVN at HUROIR re leaving Men Covering to	FfR
"	18		Adam & Soyers stoves & places hrs at Battle of GERMAINE.	FfR
"	19		Issued new rifles, rifle bonds, bayonets to attack when floury nordes.	FfR
"	20		Rode to HUROIR selected Site for stores.	FfR
"	21		Visited ADOS 4 Corp.	

Army Form C. 2118.

WAR DIARY
or
INTELLIGENCE SUMMARY.
(Erase heading not required.)

DADOS 61st DIV.
April 1917
Page 3

Place	Date	Hour	Summary of Events and Information	Remarks and references to Appendices
VIGNACOURT	1917 April 22		Moved to BAVOUR & pitched Camp	t/f R.
MIRAUMONT	23		Arranged to refill hearts & informed all concerned. N. Kitchen prevented us but whilst DADOS & Corps in Reorgln. informed that it was unnecessary.	t/f R.
"	24		Sent lorry to HERBONNIERES to collect huts & stoves from Salvage to complete Division. Visits ADOS & Corps.	t/f R.
"	25			
"	26		Wired for 18pr Gun to replace screws A/306 RFA. Sent 9 Travel Covers to 61 BAC urgently required on trip, had been ordered to relieve Cellars owing to danger.	

Harry Jameson Black Capt. ADOS

D.A.D.O.S.
61st DIVN.
1 MAY 1917

Vol 13

WAR DIARY

DADOS - 61st DIVISION

May 1917

WAR DIARY

AA&QA 61st Dvn.

INTELLIGENCE SUMMARY

(Erase heading not required.)

Army Form C. 2118.

May 1917

Place	Date	Hour	Summary of Events and Information	Remarks and references to Appendices
FORESTE	1917 May 1	—	18 pr Lim BM for M730 received & issued to 10M pr filling	A&R
"	2	—	Ammunition 1 Lewis Gun to replace one lost in action by 2/4 Ox & Bucks LI, who at the same have captured 3 German machine guns	A&R
"	3	—	Visited AADOS 32 Divn. ADOS TO Corps & Salvage Dump VOYENNES	A&R
"	5	—	Received Lewis Gun spr 2/4 Ox & Bucks LI. Demanded 16 pr pn A/307 to replace "U". Received a number of Steel helmets with curtains - Several cases of returns for filling in ammunition slips - Replied in matter to Q. I suggests the ammunition was not welcomed by the troops, in the amount of time to be expended in ammunition slips named in way of further demands.	A&R
"	7	—	Inspected stores of various units - ADOS enquires what numbers of 18 pr lubin h&R I in possession - Replied "Nil".	A&R
"	9	—	Wires ADOS estimate of No. of trench requiring water clothing. Received notification that such clothing to be withdrawn - saw Q. - arranged	A&R
"	10	—	Put revise Order firing date - Arranged dump p in reception On ADOS' instruction sent 3 lorries to HARBONNIERES to evacuate Divn. Reserve of SD clothing.	A&R

Army Form C. 2118.

Page 2.

WAR DIARY
INTELLIGENCE SUMMARY
(Erase heading not required.)

Instructions regarding War Diaries and Intelligence Summaries are contained in F. S. Regs., Part II. and the Staff Manual respectively. Title pages will be prepared in manuscript.

Place	Date	Hour	Summary of Events and Information	Remarks and references to Appendices
FORESTE.	1917 May 10.	—	Received verbal instructions from Q. that helmets fitted with steel curtains to be issued, but no eskdowns to be fitted in Armourers' Shop.	K+R.
"	11	—	Received warnings re Armourers Shop leaving shortly moving north. Moved Armourers Shop to NESLE when the Sector Stores Tent. Received Travel Schedule for returning Winter Clothing — Impossible to comply with same as Area runs to clear when 2 days before being taken over by K. Arenol. Phoned ATDD, who replies "Make own arrangement". Wire Base to Inspence all issues from 14th inst. Saw A.D.O. Neele on afterwards Q.61 & drafted DRO instructing all units to hand in Winter Clothing on 12 and 13th. Arranged also Area Stores Dump to Salvage Officer for receipt from all Area Stores.	K+R K+R
"	12			
"	13		Winter Clothing arrivis in fair — Held first day's hand of stores on same. Sent 14 lorry loads winter clothing to Railhead, shoes & overshoes. Men employed 4 a.m. to 11 p.m. Held second day's hand, reminded of clothing having come in.	K+R

T2134. Wt. W708-776. 500000. 4/15. Sir J. C. & S.

Army Form C. 2118.

WAR DIARY
INTELLIGENCE SUMMARY
(Erase heading not required.)

Page 3.

Place	Date	Hour	Summary of Events and Information	Remarks and references to Appendices
FORESTE	1917 MAY 14	—	Sent 10 lorry loads unserviceable stores, also 4 lorry loads unserviceable stores. Infantry Divn Stores Dump, & informed ABPO that 100 Packages were being returned to Base also No. of Telf. Mullers Coy to Conf: Troops.	K.H.R.
"	15	—	Wired Base to resume issue 19th inst. A lorry was sent to Durand Brawnser stores to Railhead. Dump inspected by Durand of Brawnser. Should not of Serv: Infuriation to many Commanders. "Moved" 61 San Sect to 66 IV Army Group.	K.H.R.
"	"	"	" 32 " " 6 Padded 32nd Div.	K.H.R.
"	16	—	Inspected Salvage & Area Stores Dump. Moved on 4 lorry loads to VIGNACOURT, arrived 4.30 p.m. Pitched Camp.	K.H.R.
VIGNACOURT	17	1 am	Despatched 2 lorries to fetch Ammunition from NESLE.	K.H.R.
"	19	—	Received warning order Ammunition wanted 21st.	K.H.R.
"	20	—	Received 6 tons clothing boots &c. Did not arrive in time of move.	K.H.R.
"	21	—	Moves to DOULLENS. 8 lorry loads. Durand Brawnser for distinguishing ambulance. Moves Base ungoing.	K.H.R.

WAR DIARY or INTELLIGENCE SUMMARY

Army Form C. 2118.

Page 4

Place	Date	Hour	Summary of Events and Information	Remarks and references to Appendices
DOULLENS	1917 May 22	—	Base replied that no cloth was available. On G.O.C's instructions the necessary amount was purchased, as it was imperative that troops should have the cloth before arrival in new area.	
"	23	8 am	Moved to LE CAUROY.	K+R
LE CAUROY	24	9 am	Moved to WARLUS. Pitched Camp. Informed DADOS III Army & ADOS VI Corps of arrival, with position of Stores & Office: also sent ADOS quant'y of information wanted required.	K+R
WARLUS			25 Ton Stores arrived from HAVRE; borrowed & additional lorries released same. Arranged refilling for tomorrow.	K+R
"	26	—	Visited 61 DIV. ARTILLERY at OCCOCHES & arranged to refill them tomorrow.	K+R
"	27	—	Sent 4 lorry loads Stores to DIV. ARTILLERY.	
"	28	—	3 Light T. Mortars received for 182 T.M. B'ty in replacement of 3 with FOULIS MORTARS.	
"	29	—	Went to 3 ARMY GUN PARK & drew 2 Vickers Guns for 183 M.G. Coy.	
"	30	—	Visited 61 DIV. ARTILLERY. Warning Order Division moves to ARRAS 2nd prox.	
"	31	—	Went BARRAS. Saw DADOS 37 DIVN re taking over. Went to VI Corps HQ in place of ADOS on leave.	

A. Scanghrave & Roberts Capt

DADOS 61st DIVN.   2nd June 1917.

WAR DIARY

D.A.D.O.S. 61st DIVN

JUNE 1917

VOL. XIV

Army Form C. 2118.

WAR DIARY

June 1917
DADOS. 61st DIVN.
INTELLIGENCE SUMMARY.
Page 1.
(Erase heading not required.)

Instructions regarding War Diaries and Intelligence Summaries are contained in F. S. Regs., Part II. and the Staff Manual respectively. Title pages will be prepared in manuscript.

Place	Date	Hour	Summary of Events and Information	Remarks and references to Appendices
WARLUS.	June 1917 1st	—	Two 14" shells from German Naval Gun fell within 150 yds of my Stores. No damage done.	
"	2nd	—	Made further arrangement with DADOS. 37 DIV re taking over in ARRAS. Went to VI Corps for an hour to ask for ADOS. Moved to ARRAS taking over from 37th DIVN for ammunition 5 Brigades of Artillery and 20 other attached units. Cleared 16 tons from Railhead.	K&R
ARRAS.	3rd	—	Collected 18 pr M/a BM for attached Battery. Went VI Corps to ask for ADOS. Railhead shells — Saw 10M No 25 Workshop AOD — Went VI Corps to ask for ADOS	K&R K&R
"	4th	—	Visited VI Corps Ammunition Shop: arranges relief of 37 DIVL Armourers by Armourers of 3rd Division. Went VI Corps to ask for ADOS.	K&R
"	5th	—	Went to Army Gunpark at FREVENT to arrange about Stores. Went to VI Corps to ask for ADOS.	
"	6th	—	Visited Brigade Ammunition Shops. Went to VI Corps to ask for ADOS	K&R
"	7th	—	Received small quantity Service cdn Leather for Division — Shortage badly felt — Arranges with G.O.C. to break in future. Wrote to DIV HQrs re Ordnance Services to WD. XIX Corps troops	K&R

WAR DIARY
INTELLIGENCE SUMMARY.
(Erase heading not required.)

June 1917
DADOS 61. DIVN
Page 2.

Army Form C. 2118.

Place	Date	Hour	Summary of Events and Information	Remarks and references to Appendices
ARRAS	June 1917 8th	—	ADOS having returned from leave, I took him on several matters. Warning order received that Division moves to WARLUS on 11th. Made arrangements accordingly.	K+R
"	9th		Saw DADOS 56th DIVN re handing over.	K+R
"	10th		Went to WARLUS to arrange for Camp.	K+R
"	11th		Moved Armourers Shop & Gas Stores to WARLUS.	K+R
"			Moved to WARLUS. Handed over all stores etc. up to 56th DIVN, &	
WARLUS	12th		took over 61st DIVN ARTY from O.O. XIX Corps Troops.	K+R
"	13th		Took over a number of stores land made from other formations.	K+R
"	13th		Visited Q.M Stores 182 Infantry Bde.	K+R
"	14th		" " 183 "	K+R
"	15th		" " 184 "	K+R
"	16th		" DIVL ARTILLERY.	K+R
"	17th		Armourer S. Sergt STANLEY called in to talk over DIVL ARMRS SHOP	
"			Vice from QMS Schofield who went to H.Q. 184 Infantry Bde. Purchased 35 Kilos Service oil in paint, varnish, repairs.	K+R
"	19th		Received warning Division moves to unknown area on 21st. Suspended all moves from Base.	K+R

WAR DIARY
INTELLIGENCE SUMMARY

Army Form C. 2118.

June 1917
Appx. 61st Div.
P. 3

Place	Date	Hour	Summary of Events and Information	Remarks and references to Appendices
WARLUS	June 1917 20.	—	Saw ADDs T/Corps re moving Divl Arty & obtained troops to then formations. Necessary orders taken. Artillery being moved to 56th Divn.	AtR
"	21	—	Visited WILLEMAN. Selected site for camp.	AtR
"	22	—	Sent Armourer's Park forward to such camp. Removed superstructures & issues from Baden.	AtR
"	23	—	Moved to WILLEMAN. Visit DDOS III Army asking him if this was in his area & if so location of nearest workshops.	AtR
WILLEMAN	24	—	Visited Brigade & RE areas and arranged refilling points & men to Infantry Brigade Ammunition Shops.	AtR
"	25	—	No reply having been received from DDOS III Army, scoured country. Search of Workshops, found No. 18 & 31 at REBREUVE and 14 & 19 at ST POL. Got Q to wire for authority to use these for refuns to Waterlot at Wilchem & inform me. 3 Army State refuns can be effected at Nos 18 & 31 Workshops. Drafted DRO accordingly.	AtR
"	26	—	Visited Armourers. Reconnoitred strength including Service Ammn Paws to 56th Divn. for 61st DIVL ARTILLERY.	AtR
"	27	—		

WAR DIARY
or
INTELLIGENCE SUMMARY. DADOS. 61. DIV.

June 1917
N. 4

Army Form C. 2118.

Place	Date	Hour	Summary of Events and Information	Remarks and references to Appendices
WILLEMAN	June 1917 28		Called for return from 3 Inf. Bdes as to nos. of special articles in possession due in Indent.	Kyf Kyk
	29.		Went on leave	

K. Macpherson Grant
Capt AOO.
DADOS 61st DIVN
29/6/17
17/6/17

WAR DIARY

D.A.D.O.S. 61st DIVISION.

July 1917.

Vol. XV

Army Form C. 2118.

WAR DIARY
INTELLIGENCE SUMMARY.
(Erase heading not required)

DADOS 61st DIVN. Page 1.
JULY, 1917.

Instructions regarding War Diaries and Intelligence Summaries are contained in F.S. Regs., Part II. and the Staff Manual respectively. Title pages will be prepared in manuscript.

Place	Date	Hour	Summary of Events and Information	Remarks and references to Appendices
	1917. JULY			
WILLEMAN	1	-	251 Employment Coy want stores, having just formed division. Wrote III Army for scale.	
"	2	-	III Army Gun Park at FREVENT closed. Indents transferred to Gun Park at ALBERT. Waterrant for 2/7 WARWICKS, K.T. Body for 2/1 BUCKS received.	
"			B.W.R. returns for lost equipt. sent to III Army.	
"			Having ascertained differences in special stores held by unit. Informed Q.61	
"	4	-	Wires for Wagon Limbered RE for 476 Field Coy RE.	
"	5	-	Wired for K.T. Body for 2/5 GLOSTERS.	
"	7	-	Lorry collected stores from Gun Park at ALBERT. News lactometer last received. 61 DIV ART now at FREVENT but waiting hotter. Wagon Limbered RE for 476 Fld Coy + K.T. Body for 2/5 GLOSTERS recd.	
"	8		Four attached men returned to units.	
"	9		Returned from leave. Above entries received from School lr.	K.T.R.
"	10		Visited H.Q. 61 RA. at ST. POL separate required to complete Limbers loaned to INF. BDES. Arranged for 61 DIV ART. to hold same pending return to them of the limbers.	K.T.R.
"	11			K.T.R.
"	12		Received quartery of S.C. Paint sufficient to meet demands of Divn. to date. Informed Q. 61	

T:134. Wt. W708—776. 500000. 4/16. Sir J. C. & S.

Army Form C. 2118.

WAR DIARY
INTELLIGENCE SUMMARY
(Erase heading not required)

DADOS 61st DIVN Page 2
JULY 1917

Instructions regarding War Diaries and Intelligence Summaries are contained in F. S. Regs, Part II. and the Staff Manual respectively. Title pages will be prepared in manuscript.

Place	Date	Hour	Summary of Events and Information	Remarks and references to Appendices
WILLEMAN	1917 JULY 13	—	Received wire from XIX Corp Troops telling me to transfer to DIV. ARTY to whom Replies now endorsed by 56 DIVN, to whom were has been referred	K.R.
"	16	—	Received Verbal intimation Divn. moves shortly after 21st inst. Wired Ordnance HAVRE ROUEN & CALAIS, making necessary arrangements. Wired GUN PARK ALBERT that I any issues call to collect all outstanding stores, on 19th inst.	K.R.
"	17	—	Received verbal intimation Divisional start moving 25th inst certain. Wired 3 Bases that stores cannot be accepted after 23rd inst.	K.R.
"	19	—	Collected outstanding stores from GUN PARK ALBERT & issued same.	K.R.
"	20	—	Wrote HAVRE & ROUEN that all outstanding indents should now be transferred to CALAIS. Wrote CALAIS with last of indents & full explanations. Horse shoes h&R. received — this being last B.w.R. received prior to move. No destination (except V Army area), after move, yet known. 175 sets Pack Saddlery issued to 3 INF. Bdes.	K.R.

Army Form C. 2118.

WAR DIARY

INTELLIGENCE SUMMARY
(Erase heading not required)

Instructions regarding War Diaries and Intelligence Summaries are contained in F. S. Regs., Part II. and the Staff Manual respectively. Title pages will be prepared in manuscript.

DADS.
61st DIVN   Page 3.
JULY 1917

Place	Date	Hour	Summary of Events and Information	Remarks and references to Appendices
WILLEMAN	1917 JULY 21	—	III Army wired that use of A.G. Goggles be discontinued & all to be withdrawn. All units wired to return same. Outstanding indents cancelled.	K&R.
"	22 & 23	—	All units visited & instructed regarding return of all unserviceable stores & men to make. Also statements obtained from all that transport complete and ready to move.	K&R
"	24	—	Collected all A.G. Goggles & despatched same to Base.	K&R
"	25	—	Dismounted part of band preparatory to moving tomorrow.	K&R.
"	26	9.30 am	Moved off in 4 lorries to ZEGGAR'S CAPEL.	
ZEGGAR'S CAPEL	"	4.30	Arrived and pitched camp — all complete by 8 P.M. Ascertained tactical position & wired CMLM's am now in position to receive. Notified DADS V Army & Asst VIII Corps position of stores & office. Sent ADOS various returns & information urgently required on journey here today.	K&R
"	27	"	Field allotted to me for camp being too small, moved camp to another. Field a short distance away.	
"	27	"	Wrote DDOS, I Army & collected 29 Compasses magnetic.	K&R

Army Form C. 2118.

DADOS 61st DIVN Page 4

WAR DIARY
INTELLIGENCE SUMMARY.
JULY 1917

(Erase heading not required.)

Instructions regarding War Diaries and Intelligence Summaries are contained in F.S. Regs., Part II. and the Staff Manual respectively. Title pages will be prepared in manuscript.

Place	Date	Hour	Summary of Events and Information	Remarks and references to Appendices
ZEGGARS CAPEL	1917 JULY 28	—	Visited HQ 183 INF BDE. Thread refilling point.	WD
"	29	—	" 182 & 184 " "	WD
"	30	—	First consignment of stores from CHATS	WD
"	31	—	Visited RED ARNEKE, ADO 8 Corps, 10M MT Workshop. In addition to above, usual routine visits were made to units, Salvage Dump, Brigade Armourers' Shops, etc.	WD

K. Stephenson (Lt. AOD)

D.A.D.O.S. 61st DIVN.
2 AUG 1917

Vol/6

WAR DIARY.
DADOS. 61st DIVN.
AUGUST 1917
Vol. XVI

Army Form C. 2118.

WAR DIARY
INTELLIGENCE SUMMARY.
(Erase heading not required.)

RA.DOS. 61. DIV.
AUGUST, 1917.
PAGE. 1.

Instructions regarding War Diaries and Intelligence Summaries are contained in F. S. Regs., Part II. and the Staff Manual respectively. Title pages will be prepared in manuscript.

Place	Date	Hour	Summary of Events and Information	Remarks and references to Appendices
ZEGGERS CAPPEL	1917 AUG. 1	—	At request of ADOS of Army furnished him with a list of all local purchases made from this Division since January 1917.	KtR
"	2	—	Reft to Ring required for making Haversacks slings Bandoliers same from Base.	KtR
"	3	—	Visited various units of 182 INF BDE regarding equipment	KtR
"	4	—	" " " 183 " " " "	KtR
"	5	—	" Ordnance CALAIS on various matters	KtR
"	6	—	" 184 INF. Workshop on various matters	KtR
"	7	—	Reft for Haversacks slings received and issued.	KtR
"	8	—	ADOS VIII Corps called on various Stores. ADOS XIX Corps enquires whether Divison was equipped ready to scale. Replied yes, with exception of Revolvers, 531 of which were due out. Ill in bed.	KtR KtR
"	9-12	—	Attended Division Q Conference & reported on state of equipment of the Division.	KtR KtR
"	13	—	Received notice Division moves to POPERINGHE on 15th inst.	KtR KtR
"	15	—	Moves to POPERINGHE.	KtR

WAR DIARY
or
INTELLIGENCE SUMMARY.
(Erase heading not required.)

Army Form C. 2118.

DADOS 61 DIVN
AUGUST 1917
Page 2.

Place	Date	Hour	Summary of Events and Information	Remarks and references to Appendices
POPERINGHE	1917 AUG. 16	-	Visited 1/5 BTLN 1/6th & 164 INF BDE and MERSEA CAMP	K+R
	17	-	Division moved to MERSEA CAMP Formerly — Arranged to take over Jumieres	K+R
			adjoining Ten Elms Camp now occupied by DADOS 36 DIVN	
	18		Moved to TEN ELMS CAMP, where POPERINGHE Informed ADDS XIX	K+R
			Corps & BDES & Army new location	
	19		Visited 2/6 WARWICKS, 154 BHQ, 1/2 3d AMBCE	K+R
	20		BHQ, Boulstone, Salvage Officer 164 Bde, Transport, 2/4 Oxfords.	K+R
	21		Moved 36 DIV ARTY Camp to 36 DIV for Ordnance of hat fur	K+R
			Camps, HAVRE & ROUEN as 36 DIV moves to 3 Army Area (Southern Base)	
	22		55 DIV ARTY moves to us for Ordnance	K+R
			Visited 61 Suffk Cd. HQ 2nd Aug 61, 1, & 61 DAC.	L+L
	23		HQ 55 DIV ARTY	L+L
	24		Local purchases in DUNKERQUE	K+L
	25		Visited Champ Gun Park, 10M M10 E3, Rue POPERINGHE	
	26		Visited Camps & Obtained 350 suits SD clothing for each Bn of 183 INF BDE	K+L
			coming out of line on 30t.	

WAR DIARY

INTELLIGENCE SUMMARY

DADOS. 61 DIV
AUG. 1917.
Page 3.

Army Form C. 2118.

Place	Date	Hour	Summary of Events and Information	Remarks and references to Appendices
PERONNE	1917 AUG 29		Visit to B/308 -	KR
	30.		Army Pm Appx XIX Conf. G.O.C. during his absence on leave. G.O.C. 61 DIV inspected my department stores &	KR
	31		Returning from Appx XIX Conf. Visited HQrs V Army.	KR

General note on Month -
Large demands or orders during billet hard Remarks. Army to advise Operations - Issue of Gun Howitzers Vickers & Lewis Guns as follows :-
  2 - 15" Guns
  6 - do Carriages
  1 - 4.5 Hows
  1 - " Carriage
  24 Lewis Guns,
  9 Vickers Guns.

[signature]

D.A.D.O.S. 61st DIVN.
1 SEP 1917

WAR DIARY

D.A.D.O.S. 61st DIVISION

SEPTEMBER 1917

VOL XVII

D.A.D.O.S. 61st DIVN.
1 OCT 1917

Army Form C. 2118.

WAR DIARY
DADOS 61st Div
INTELLIGENCE SUMMARY
SEPT. 1917.
(Erase heading not required.)

Instructions regarding War Diaries and Intelligence Summaries are contained in F. S. Regs., Part II. and the Staff Manual respectively. Title pages will be prepared in manuscript.

Place	Date	Hour	Summary of Events and Information	Remarks and references to Appendices
POPERINGHE	Sept 1	—	Acting for ADOS XIX Corps during his absence.	
	2	—	Received Returned 3 Lewis Guns to 2/5 GLOSTER REGT.	W.R.
	3	—	Acting for ADOS XIX Corps	W.R.
	4	—	Do. Vickers Pul. Stores Salvage	W.R.
	5	—	Do. Vickers Gun Parts	W.R.
"	6	—	Received 18/pr complete for A/306. airplane destroyed in action	W.R.
"	7	—	Had limber/harness at DUNKERQUE.	W.R.
"	8	—	Received 18/pr without BM for 19/307. airplane burnt	W.R.
"	9	—	Received VICKERS GUN complete for 183 Bde M.G. Coy airplane destroyed in action	W.R.
"		—	Vickers ADOS II Corps also herewith Vickers etc from ADOS XIX Corps	W.R.
"		—	D.W.O. re Various area Stores	W.R.
"	11	—	Received new Pattern Greys Ammn. for ARTILLERY	W.R.
"		—	Received warning from Q that Divnroom slack moving to III Corps area on 13th	
			Wires HAYRE suspending issue, & notified all concerned re change of Base from Mark to South. Sent list forward to all concerned.	W.R.

T2134. Wt. W708—776. 500000. 4/15. Sir J. C. & S.

Army Form C. 2118.

WAR DIARY or INTELLIGENCE SUMMARY

(Erase heading not required.)

DADOS 61. DIV.N SEPT. 1917 Page 2.

Place	Date	Hour	Summary of Events and Information	Remarks and references to Appendices
POPERINGHE	Sept 12	-	New CRMS to collect special issue of S.D. clothing	KR
"	13	-	Received 16/4 + BM for 13/306, uniform issued	KR
"	14	-	Received 1 Lewis gun for 2/6 WARWICKS replace destroyed	KR
"	15	-	Arranged with DADOS 55 DIVN re handing over dump & certain stores to him	KR
WATOU	16	-	Thoroughly cleaned up office block & put everything standing over	KR
"	17	-	Moved to WATOU and pitched Camp. Arranged refilling tomorrow	KR
"	18	-	Moved by road to DUISANS - were given III Army DADOS XVII Corps new location	KR
"	19	-	Remarks from Base 1 blanket per man, 1 Rug per horse, on ration strength	KR
"	20	-	Warning received that DIVN moves to ARRAS (St NICHOLAS) on 25th inst.	KR
"	21	-	Visited DADOS 17 DIVN at OIL FACTORY, St NICHOLAS to arrange taking over	KR
"	22	-	ADOS XVII Corps called	KR
"	23	-	Visited DADOS 17 DIVN	KR
"	24	-	Made all arrangements for move tomorrow	KR
"	25	-	Move to ARRAS (St NICHOLAS): has place thoroughly cleaned out	KR
"	26	-	Visited Railhead Salvage & unit	KR
ARRAS	27	-	Received all stores/rugs (4000) & issued same	KR

WAR DIARY
INTELLIGENCE SUMMARY
(Erase heading not required.)

Army Form C. 2118.

DADOS 61 DIV
SEPT. 1917.
P. 3.

Place	Date	Hour	Summary of Events and Information	Remarks and references to Appendices
ARRAS	SEPT 23	—	Received 1 Lewis gun for 2/6 Warwicks, replace destroyed	
			" " " 2/1 Bucks "	
			" " " 3 " "	
			Returned School.	
	30	—	100 Yukon Packs from Base.	K.R.L.
			To date, out of 16,000 blankets demanded 15550 received. Drawers & new SRD invoices stating that DWI Batts only can draw not issued. Drawn under orders to replace dirty or unserviceable articles. Infants must be sent to me to effect exchange with full explanation. Received warning that three of my Category A A.S.C. men should be relieved by B Category men.	
			Public RADOS 12 and 15 DIVNS	K.R.L.

D.A.D.O.S.
61st DIVN.
1 OCT 1917

Vol 18

WAR DIARY.
D.A.D.O.S. 61st DIVN
October 1917
Vol. XVIII

D.A.D.O.S.
61st DIVN.
4 NOV 1917

Army Form C. 2118.

ARDOS
61st DW

WAR DIARY

INTELLIGENCE SUMMARY.

OCTOBER 1917.

(Erase heading not required.)

Instructions regarding War Diaries and Intelligence
Summaries are contained in F. S. Regs., Part II.
and the Staff Manual respectively. Title pages
will be prepared in manuscript.

Place	Date	Hour	Summary of Events and Information	Remarks and references to Appendices
ST. NICHOLAS ARRAS.	1917 Oct. 1	—	Visited Salvage & Ord Laundry reference return of underclothing.	KAR
"	2	—	Drafted further DRO on the subject of Laundry supplies. Visited 182 Bde HQ in the time. Returned 150 sets Paillasses & 5 & 17 cwt Trs.	KAR
"	3	—	Dismantled 1 Lewis gun pin 2/4 Ox Bucks L.I. to reform U.	KAR
"	5	—	Visited 184 Bde Battalion.	KAR
"	5	—	Advance completed with 1 Battalion men.	KAR
"	5	—	8 Double sets R.D. Harness in hand with Kitchen oven from 17 D.W. in saddle	KAR
"	6	—	on vans, sent to Base with explanation.	KAR
"	8	—	2 o/m Lewis Gun butt received. Selected new site for Stores in ARRAS. Sent Carpenters to make	KAR
"	13	—	alterations & carry out repairs. On Mil Army authority asked 4 six inch Newton TM from Park. Stakens all made so submerine fastened to wooden shelving.	KAR KAR
"	15	—	Demanded 2 m Hawkins mine pr Division. Moved into Rue Baudimont, ARRAS.	KAR
"	20	—	Went on leave to England. (10 days)	KAR

T2134. Wt. W708—776. 500000. 4/15. Sir J. C. & S.

WAR DIARY

INTELLIGENCE SUMMARY

Army Form C. 2118.

ADM 61 DIV
Oct 1917
Page 2

Place	Date	Hour	Summary of Events and Information	Remarks and references to Appendices
MERAS	1917 Oct 21	—	18,000 Blankets (lung 2nd pr wan) received & issued. Ammunition inspected after 3 2/4 Warwick. Demanded 1 Lewis Gun for 2/4 Gloster. Reference deficiencies	WR
"	"		Inspection of Ammunition called & arranged to inspect Rifles & Machine Guns of 182 INF BDE	
"	22		Coinage for two escapees in Billet issues to ORE	WR
"	24		3804 pr Boots TB received & issued	WR
"	25		11,300 pr Drawers woollen received & issued. 6,500 Leather Jerkins. 3500 fur undercoats received for Infantry	WR
"	26		Progress report on winter clothing sent to Q. 61 Div.	WR
"	27		Form 6" "New Sub" TM received & issued	WR
"	28		Under Corps instructions Collected Serviceable tents from Camps.	WR
"	30		Attended DHQ with ADOS XVII Corps re Ordnance matters - DHQ expressed themselves as quite satisfied	WR

R. Dampremain Capt.
ADOS 61 DIV. 4/11/17

VOL 19

WAR DIARY.

DAROS. 61st DIVN.

NOVEMBER 1917.

VOL. XIX.

Army Form C. 2118.

WAR DIARY

DADOS
61. DIVN
Nov. 1917.

INTELLIGENCE SUMMARY.
(Erase heading not required.)

Instructions regarding War Diaries and Intelligence Summaries are contained in F.S. Regs., Part II. and the Staff Manual respectively. Title pages will be prepared in manuscript.

Place	Date	Hour	Summary of Events and Information	Remarks and references to Appendices
ARRAS	1917 Nov 2	-	Returned from leave.	Ap1
	3	-	Engaged forgeover Downmentry	Ap2
	4	-	ditto	Ap2
	5	-	ADOS 17 Corps ill. Systematic personal inspection of all M6 rifles started	Ap4
	7	-	Arranged inspection of 184 SA by A.I.A.	Ap2
	8	-	Settled various matters re French Area Stores	Ap2
	9	-	Saw 10M & 86 guns same time 306 Bde RFA voters on 14th	Ap2
	10	-	AM. Salvage started smelly reg. soldier from Bully Beef tins - Very satisfactory results.	Ap2
	11	-	Saw Salvage, Bailleul 7 16.3 Bde.	Ap9
	12	-	Bought 200 lamps for Trucks. Home today arrived from Base.	Ap1
	13	-	Movies 306 Bde RFA to IV Corps T Subdep.	Ap1.C
	14	-	On a Commandment inspected Billets	Ap1
	16	-	Large numbers of Trucks, also 6 luminous watches, bought for new	Ap1
	18	-	Inspection of M.G. & S.A. of 183 Inf. Bde completed.	Ap1
	20	-	Division reports Pack horse Saddles for Weblers Guns - Obtain Carpenters material	Ap2
			Works B turn out 150.	Ap2

T2134. Wt. W708–776. 500000. 4/15. Sir J. C. & S.

Army Form C. 2118.

WAR DIARY

BATOS 61 DIV.

INTELLIGENCE SUMMARY
(Erase heading not required)

NOV 1917   Page 2.

Instructions regarding War Diaries and Intelligence Summaries are contained in F. S. Regs., Part II. and the Staff Manual respectively. Title pages will be prepared in manuscript.

Place	Date	Hour	Summary of Events and Information	Remarks and references to Appendices
MKhz	1917 Nov 21	–	Arranged evacuation of MG PSA of 182 Inf Bde	Nil
	25	–	ADOS of Corps called & saw 10ᵃᵐ re Guns & Parkeagle crates. Handed fuller of Divisions type tetum, 14th & 15th DIVNS to copy. Instructions received to cancel all outstanding demands for guns on 28th & submit report	Nil
	27	–	Warning received DHN (lightly) matter KANGAM AREA 36th int Stopped all leave from Base	Nil
	30	–	Moved to GREVILLERS – Instructions otters – moved to PERONNE Rd and remained for the night	Nil

Harry Drummond Grant
Capt.
DADOS 61st DIV.

4ᵗʰ Dec. 1917.

WAR DIARY
DADOS. 61 DIVN.
DECEMBER 1917

Vol. XX

D.A.D.O.S.
61st DIVN.
4 JAN 1918

Army Form C. 2118.

WAR DIARY
INTELLIGENCE SUMMARY
(Erase heading not required.)

RA ADS. 61st DIV
Dec. 1917.

Instructions regarding War Diaries and Intelligence Summaries are contained in F.S. Regs., Part II. and the Staff Manual respectively. Title pages will be prepared in manuscript.

Place	Date	Hour	Summary of Events and Information	Remarks and references to Appendices
BEAUVENCOURT	1917 Dec 1	—	Saw ADDS + Cmdt. moved to ETRICOURT.	K.H.R.
ETRICOURT	2	—	Removed suspension from Bases. Collected 500 Belts + Braces from Gunpowder for M.G. Coys.	K.H.R.
"	3	—	Issue 100 Packsaddle crates made in Divl. Ammunition Shop.	K.H.L.
"	4	—	Inspected stores of all QMs at EQUANCOURT.	K.H.L.
"	6	—	Went to III Army Gunpark.	K.H.L.
"	12	—	Visited ADOS III Corps — re Divl. Salvage System.	K.H.L.
"	"	—	Handed over to III Army Gunpark belonging from salving by DIVN.	
"	"	—	Moved 3 lorry loads surplus stores out Camwilte to Railhead.	K.H.R.
"	13	—	Ascertained 306 Bde RFA were not getting stores from OO — Wired various D.O.S +	
"	"	—	collected lorry load from BO. I Capt Trustpe.	K.H.L.
"	14	—	No stores from Base for several days owing to breakage by Trawler.	K.H.L.
"	"	—	306 Bde RFA moves to me	K.H.L.
"	16	—	12 DIV ARTILLERY moved to me — have them again on 21st.	
"	15	—	Ascertained they were rejoining him on 21st.	K.H.L.
"	"	—	Reserves notification DIVN moves out on 23rd.	
"	"	—	Supplied 12 DIV ARY with underclothing, horseshoes stores + postnails.	K.H.R.

WAR DIARY or INTELLIGENCE SUMMARY

Army Form C. 2118.

Page 2. Dec. 1917.

Place	Date	Hour	Summary of Events and Information	Remarks and references to Appendices
ETRICOURT	1917 Dec 20	—	Divn moves to BRAY on 23rd. Shepherds issues from Base after issue.	K.R.
"	21	—	Purchases 100 kilos frost needs in AMIENS.	K.R.
"	22	—	Area Stores arrives. Shepherd over to O.D. T. Corps Transp. 40 Tons in all.	K.R.
"	23	—	Moved to MERICOURT SUR SOMME.	
"	26	—	Commences Brigades re refitting in Special Stores.	K.R.
"	27	—	General instruction re frost cups. Moves Base for supply.	K.R.
"	28	—	Purchase frost needs in AMIENS. DIVN march to HARBONNIERES 31 Dec.	K.R.
"	29	—	Collects frost cups from 80 XVIII Corps Transp.	K.R.
"	30	—	Frost cup received from Base.	K.R.
"	31	—	Moves to HARBONNIERES.	K.R.

General Note. Purchases of frost cups insufficient. Suggest Toffee Stores be supplied all the year round, & frost cups be supplied in half standard of each Divn at end of Oct each year, in addition to supplies coming up with Stores.

K.R. Stewart Capt.
ADDS 61 DIV

YA 21

WAR DIARY

D.A.D.O.S. 61st DIVN.

JANUARY 1918

Vol. XXI

Army Form C. 2118.

WAR DIARY
INTELLIGENCE SUMMARY
(Erase heading not required)

DADOS 61st DIV.
JAN. 1917

Instructions regarding War Diaries and Intelligence Summaries are contained in F. S. Regs., Part II. and the Staff Manual respectively. Title pages will be prepared in manuscript.

Place	Date	Hour	Summary of Events and Information	Remarks and references to Appendices
HARBONNIÈRES	1919			
	1/1	—	Informed XVIII Corps numbers of 18th & 4.5" Hows outstanding	K.A.R.
"	2/1	—	Wrote Q - 61 Div & Corps re provision of area stores in next area	K.A.R.
"	3/1	—	XVIII Corps called	
			Division moves on 7th to NESLE. Suspended issues after 4.5	K.A.R.
"	4/1		3rd K. Dvn. Called re taking over premises	K.A.R.
"	7/1		Moved to NESLE	K.A.R.
NESLE	9/1		Purchase re Headquarters for divisional staff tables	K.A.R.
"	10/1		Went to AVROIR re taking over SOS, park on to construct stores	K.A.R.
"	11/1		Moved certain stores KAVROIR & collected area stores from HAM	K.A.R.
"	12/1		Moved to AVROIR - Collected 2 - 18 pdrs from BAPAUME - FRENCH	
AVROIR	14/1		Took over stores at FORESTE RAILHEAD from FRENCH	K.A.R.
"	15/1		Transfers of stores at Railhead to R.S.O.	K.A.R.
			There previously	K.A.R.
"	17/1		Bde Orderly killed up 10 18 pdr Ott. Sent to workshop MATIGNY	K.A.R.
"	18/1		Called on ADOS XVIII Corps at HAM	K.A.R.
"	21/1		Thur precautions of − Collected stores from HAM & Gunpark ALBERT	K.A.R.

Army Form C. 2118.

WAR DIARY
DADOS 61 DIV
or
INTELLIGENCE SUMMARY.   JAN. 1916
(Erase heading not required.)

Instructions regarding War Diaries and Intelligence Summaries are contained in F.S. Regs., Part II. and the Staff Manual respectively. Title pages will be prepared in manuscript.

Place	Date	Hour	Summary of Events and Information	Remarks and references to Appendices
	1916			
AUBOIR	2/1	—	18/m Carriage for A9/307 received & issued	K&R
"	"	—	1 Clerk & 3 storemen to be held in readiness for short attachment to Corps Troops.	
"	23/1	—	Two 18/m pieces collected from Gun Park & taken to Working Station.	"K&R"
"	27/1	—	Received notification from ADOS XVIII Corps that I am to proceed on 29th inst to No 14 Ord Depot for a fortnight's Ammunition Course.	K&R
"	29/1	—	Left for Ammunition Course at No 14 Ordnance Depot. (1 fortnight)	K&R

[signature]
Capt
DADOS. 61 DIV

D.A.D.O.S.
61st DIVN.

YA 22

WAR DIARY

DADOS. 61st DIVISION.

FEB! 1918.

VOL. XXII

WAR DIARY

INTELLIGENCE SUMMARY

(Erase heading not required.)

Army Form C. 2118.

DADOS
61st DIVN.
Feb 1918

Place	Date	Hour	Summary of Events and Information	Remarks and references to Appendices
PURPUR	1/2/18	-	Received intimation to Battalions leaving Durban, 3 January instructions re Railway in Stores	K.H.C.
"	2	-	Arrange with unit being disbanded to bring in Stores, on a programme ADVS XVIII Corps called	K.H.K.
"	3	-	Labor Coys arriving - Instructions received to advance.	K.H.K.
"	4	-	Received stores from 5 disbanded units. Instructions to Base Vouchers is it	K.H.C.
"	5/9	-	Special stores being Reft. for DADS	K.H.C.
"	9/10	-	2 Motor Labor units arrived - Instructions forwarded regarding Quarters of Shelters received for Area Commandant	K.H.C. K.H.K.
"	15	-	12 Six inch Newton TMs moved to Durban.	K.H.K.
"	-	-	Authority received for issue of 29 tons Iron to Durban for Anti Aircraft purposes - Drew present same	K.H.C. K.H.K.
"	16	-	Last Battalion to be disbanded handed in Stores	K.H.K.
"	20	-	Pioneer Battalion to be received by 1 Coy - Arranges with Battalion to take in one quarter of their Stores	K.H.C.
"	21	-	Took in Stores of Pioneer Battalion.	K.H.C.

WAR DIARY

"DADOS 61st DIV.n"

INTELLIGENCE SUMMARY

Army Form C. 2118.

Place	Date	Hour	Summary of Events and Information	Remarks and references to Appendices
AVRAIR	23/2/18	—	Arranged with Machine Gun Officer to improvise mountings for Vickers Gun alternative positions from horseshoe boxes — Armourers Shft made 24	H.S.
	25/2/18	—	trial bar to improve 6" Newton with a view to supplying improvised gun	H.K.
	26/2/18	—	Authority for issue of 1 SMLE rifle or gun to each ASC & employment Coy. Drew 5 SMLE rifles, 1 hd [illegible] from Infantry [illegible] Brigade issued Coys — instruction of proposed recipients in use of same.	H.K.

General Note:

During month a dozen applications of kinds regarding Salvage has had a marked result, especially in regards return of old clothing.

All arrangements regarding Bathing in [illegible] of surplus equipment of [illegible] battalions have been carefully attended to the Armoured Armoured in excess of establishment. Very few deficiencies arising.

[signature] H. Humphries Smith Capt
DADOS 61st Div.

D. A. D.O.S.
61st DIV.N
3 MAR 1918

WAR DIARY.

DADOS 61st DIV

March 1918

VOL. XXIII

WAR DIARY
INTELLIGENCE SUMMARY

(Erase heading not required.)

Army Form C. 2118.

Place	Date	Hour	Summary of Events and Information	Remarks and references to Appendices
FORESTE	March 1918			
	1-5	-	Normal work	WvL
	6	-	Sir Walter Lawrence Co. arrived - Visited Works and arranged supply of necessary Ordnance Stores.	WvL
	7-15	-	Normal work	WvL
	16	-	System of Ammunition Shop in Division altered. All Armourers to come in to Divisional Armourers Shop.	WvL
	21	-	Under Divisional instructions started to move stores to RETHONVILLERS	WvL
	22	2/pm	Retreat to RETHONVILLERS, leaving 2 Warrant Officers to guard remainder of stores. These remained until 8 p.m. when the enemy were in VRAUX, 3 lorry loads of stores had to be abandoned as Ordnance lorries were required to move Div. H.Qrs.	WvL
	24	-	Retreated from RETHONVILLERS to PARVILLERS. Retreated to BEAUCOURT.	WvL WvL
	25	-		WvL
	27	-	Moves to VILLERS BRETTONEUX	WvL
	28	-	Moves to BOVES	WvL
			Obtained Machineguns & Stores from Gunpark at POIX	WvL

WAR DIARY

D.A.D.O.S. 61st DIVISION

APRIL: 1918.

V.H. XXIV

D.A.D.O.S.
61st DIVN.
1 MAY 1918

WAR DIARY
INTELLIGENCE SUMMARY.
(Erase heading not required.)

Army Form C. 2118.

DADOS 61st DIVISION
APRIL 1918
Vol. 24   Page 1

Place	Date	Hour	Summary of Events and Information	Remarks and references to Appendices
BOVES	1918 April 1	—	Received warning of move forward	KWL
"	2	—	Moves from BOVES to PISSY & billeted therein	KWL
PISSY	3	—	Move to Billet in PISSY — Ascertained units' general requirements	KWL
"	4	—	Collected Clothing, Boots, Blankets & underclothing from ABBEVILLE	KWL
"	5	—	Visits all units with underclothes, regarding repairing. Issues sufficient underclothing to give each man a clean change & sufficient S.D. Clothing & Boots to meet worst cases. Visited IV Army Gun Park	KWL KWL
"	6	—	Visited ABBEVILLE re petroleum & Machine Guns — none available	KWL
"	7	—	Ascertained from IV Army that Machine Guns may be drawn from Gun Park. Sent lorries to TREPORT for Blankets.	KWL KWL
"	8	—	Ascertained total deficiencies in Vehicles in Division & Work necessary to return Draw 141 Lewis & 30 Vickers Guns from Gun Park to complete Division. Visits Various Bos & collects Rifle Bayonet Steel Helmets & accoutrements. Received warning Division moves by train on 10th to Northern area. Informed all Bases & notified ADOS Postnam(?) (N) of present deficiencies in the Equipment of the Division	KWL

Army Form C. 2118.

DADOS. 61ST DIVN
APRIL 1916
VOL. 24. Page 2

WAR DIARY
or
INTELLIGENCE SUMMARY.
(Erase heading not required.)

Instructions regarding War Diaries and Intelligence Summaries are contained in F. S. Regs., Part II. and the Staff Manual respectively. Title pages will be prepared in manuscript.

Place	Date	Hour	Summary of Events and Information	Remarks and references to Appendices
PISSY	April 1916. 9	—	Collected all Salvage from Division & evacuated Same	K+R
"	10	—	Moved by road to HESDIN.	K+R
AIRE.	11	—	Moved by road to AIRE. Visited ADOS XI Corps, ascertained position of Gun Park.	K+R
"	12	—	Sent lorry to Gun Park for Stores, including 24 Stokes Trench Mortars	K+R
"	13	—	Went to Gun Park. Collected 28 Vickers Guns. Collected Rifles re from CCS'	K+R
"	14	—	Went to CMMS & collected flannelette, oil, field dressings, Very lights, and arranged 15 drew urgent stores by lorry.	K+R
			heavy Gun magazine being untraceable at Gun Park, sent lorry to Base for 1000.	K+R
			Lorries also Sent for Gas appliances, wire cutters re.	
"	16	—	Instructions received from XI Corps that no more lorries to go to Base without Army permission — Wired Army for permission.	K+R
"	17	8	Collected from Gun Park 13 Lewis Guns for 182 Infy Bde	K+R
"	19	—	Sent lorry to Base for Horseshoes	K+R
"	21	—	Trucks commence arriving from Base.	
"	23	—	Reported departmentally as to loss of Ordnance Stores by Division in retreat.	K+R
"	"	—	Heard that Div. Out are re-joining Div. Wired Order 56 Div asking confirmation	K+R

T2134. Wt. W708—776. 500000. 4/15. Sir J. C. & S.

WAR DIARY

A.D.O.S. 61ST DIV
April 1916

Army Form C. 2118.

INTELLIGENCE SUMMARY. Page 3

(Erase heading not required.)

Place	Date	Hour	Summary of Events and Information	Remarks and references to Appendices
MRLE	1916 April 24	–	Our 58 Div. Staff & 61 Div ARTY moved to D.O. XIX C.T. Rofz. Was talked to confirm	K&R
"	25	–	D.O. XIX C.T. Staff & 61 Div ARTY moved to D.O. XI C.T. today. Arranged with A.D.O. XI D.O. XI C.T. shewed take them on matters of D.O. XI C.T. Wires Bases	K&R
"	26	–	Sent horses to base for shoes probably required by 61 Div ARTY. Yukets all wants 61 Div ARTY stock not of deficiencies saw O.M. No 5B Workshop	K&R
"	27	–	Receives Mobilization State from 61 Div Arty. Was up for Guns & Vehicles required	K&R
"	28	–	Reviewed R.A. requests. Wired CRLMS for Vehicles & bicycles	K&R
"	29	–	Guns & Vehicles for R.A. received	
			General Note: The practice of attaching Div. Arty., when away from its Division, to the nearest D.O. is thoroughly bad. In 21 days 61 Div Arty was attached to 6 different D.O's & got no stores. A second D.O. should be appointed to each Div. to accompany it wherever under D.A.D.O.S. To accompany Div. Arty. when away from Div. & continue to administer & received stores direct from Base or DD. Div. Arty. The present system is useless from A.O. to R.A. nor A.O. Department.	
			Luck 1/5/16.	
			K Saysheamrn Brant Capt A.O.D BADOS 61st Div	

T2134. Wt. W708–776. 500000. 4/15. Sir J.C.&S.

Army Form C. 2118.

D.A.D.O.S
61. Division
May 1918

Vol 25

WAR DIARY
or
INTELLIGENCE SUMMARY.
(Erase heading not required.)

Instructions regarding War Diaries and Intelligence Summaries are contained in F.S. Regs., Part II. and the Staff Manual respectively. Title pages will be prepared in manuscript.

Place	Date	Hour	Summary of Events and Information	Remarks and references to Appendices
AIRE	1st		Saw ADOS XI Corps re issuing Ammunition to 51 & 56 OMYK Brigades. Experimental Hotchkiss MA Inspecting	
	2		D.A.D.O.S. 57 Div called for information relative to Nos. of men in 16 Div and to Calais. Received information 51 Div nos. 16 Div Artillery to be Limbers – Drawn to 18 pdr carriages	
	3		To replace 13 C/306 – continued –	
	4		16 DTMB went to 61 Div	
	5		Informed by Div Artillery moving to 4t Division	
			Sgt Desmond Infantry transferred	
	6		Number & long overtime of 66 Div following	
	7		With Gen Euringe [?]	
	8		Wrote Army Dept	
	9		Despatches on limbers, vehicles and harness 116 DAC. S+A Reply	
			before	
			Sent upload Gen and Wales for CO Clothing in	
	10		equipment – 2/4 S.H Armaments	

T.J134. Wt. W708—776. 500000. 4/15. Sir J.C. & S.

Army Form C. 2118.

WAR DIARY
or
INTELLIGENCE SUMMARY.
(Erase heading not required.)

DADOS
61 Division
May 1918

Place	Date	Hour	Summary of Events and Information	Remarks and references to Appendices
AIRE	11		Inspected 61 Div Artillery transport 4th Division horse lines	
"	12		Visited D.D.V.S. 1st Army re his recommendation re service in India	
"	13		Nil	
"	14		Nil	
"	15		Received instructions to proceed to Hesdin Ecurie to Brig Genl Up to cease Opns per Red Division ① & ② on the purposes	
"	16/17		Divt Train Remount Hors A.D.V.S. cured - Capt Nixon replaces me during relief injury to Div mounted troops to 4th Division	
"	"		Visits R.A.M.C.	
LAMBRES	18		moved to Lambres	
"	19		Met 2 61 and 51. Div Artilleries changing over lines XI and XIII Corps hr Cunfington	
"	20		61 Divl mounted troops moved home to 4th Division	

T.2134. Wt. W708—776. 500000. 4/15. Sir J. C. & S.

Army Form C. 2118.

D.A.D.O.S.
61 (2nd) Division

WAR DIARY
or
INTELLIGENCE SUMMARY.
(Erase heading not required.)

MAY 1918

Place	Date	Hour	Summary of Events and Information	Remarks and references to Appendices
LAMBRES	21		Many handovers	
	22		Received intimation from Capt. A.J. Gunn to Capt. M.D.O.S. XI Corps that District Q.M.G. instruments to be depositories of Divisional & Brigade in stationery received – Vivid ROD	
	23		Received instructions from I Army to reorganise process returns	
	24		Handovers D.A.D.O.S. & Divisions	
	25		Nil	
	26		New D. Corps. Cmd. Gardner M.D. arrived to spell handover. Division – Telephonic communication important to use hours book XI Corps G.S. 94 d/24/5/16 – Visiting ADOS.	

These are the Juniel Diaries of Capt. Davidson Roberts and Nixon from Notes left by them

[signature]

Army Form C. 2118.

DADOS
6 Division MAY 1918

WAR DIARY
or
INTELLIGENCE SUMMARY.
(Erase heading not required.)

Place	Date	Hour	Summary of Events and Information	Remarks and references to Appendices
LAMBRES	27		Visit ADOS XI Corps DDOS I Army - OO Ann MTR - Capt Nixon went on leave prior to Embarkation	
			on duty in India	
	28		Conference of Divisional OO's with ADOS. Wishes limits	
			1st Bde to more requirements of CO's	
	29		Air - Raiders and to obtain authorise in Douai in	
			case not available home Rans as been informed that Supply of	
			that - Spare part of key in repairing the Transport of hand	
			for administrative Purposes - have being inked upon Repairs	
	30		Saw Staff Captain D) 163 Bde and own arrangement made to	
			have conference with Q weekly at Headquarters	
	31		have hand over to Lt.Col I/G Royal Scots 18 Argyll & Sutherland Hldrs (Pioneers)	
			16th Division to 6th Division from 6th to 15th Division XVII Corps	

J.G.W.Armstrong
DADOS 6th Division

WAR DIARY or INTELLIGENCE SUMMARY

Army Form C. 2118.

JUNE
D.A.D.O.S.
61 DIVISION

Vol 26

Place	Date	Hour	Summary of Events and Information	Remarks and references to Appendices
LAMBRES	1.6.18		Visited by Asst D.A.D. Returned Blankets from 5 Bns and Salvage, visits Salvage dump after where there are any shirts likely to left for revision - have returned 9 Indents for Bicycles & Kitcheners motors APO 4099. 11 boxes of Nails up from Base 1/6 Camerons 18 bx 1/5th Yorkshires Highlanders sent 19 Royal Scots left 193 Bn 151st Div'n visited both Captain 193 Bn of Armed Equipment mentioned hundreds and Q'm of Oxfordshire and Bucks tradition. (reinforcement 6763) Who had one telescopic rifle Qm.	826
	2.6.18		9/11 Suffolks sent Enfd Knives bent - saw Q returned returning Lewis Gun barrels Malvein - Received of open Butt - sent nine ear-plugs leather and 1 WD of Train. Warner Kitchener repaired of timber for repairs	866
	3.		3) S.O. returned supply of Lifton winding frame (not-) - (3) Q for information they hyphens below - visiting Cavalry of Rifle pit and Thunderflasks - arranged with Q to buy some wooden stoppers in Petrol Tins	826
	3.4		Saw A.D.O.S. & discussed matters - also Q matters. Saw Q En from Brigade Corps - tried DADOS of cycles - Q M/s Supplies, Northumberland Fus. Bases 3/5 Glasters Oxfordshires. Warned Kitchener Workshops D-likeness away Road corps all supplement stokes - arranges that we have sent stokes to reconnaissance by Lorries	826

Army Form C. 2118.

WAR DIARY
or
INTELLIGENCE SUMMARY
(Erase heading not required.)

JUNE
DADOS 61 DIVN

Instructions regarding War Diaries and Intelligence Summaries are contained in F. S. Regs., Part II. and the Staff Manual respectively. Title pages will be prepared in manuscript.

Place	Date	Hour	Summary of Events and Information	Remarks and references to Appendices
LAMBRES	4.6.19		Receipt of M/ Orin	DAQ
	5.6.19		ADOS was informing us how to proceed with Supplies in DADOS cast OC G Bn R.T. Column re appearance of the intended by him Mysore, Lumps Supplementary AEO 4 Army 730. QMG 4/7 (QA3) 4/3/17, 7/3/17. OC S/L Coys with ATTACHMENT - Lung, re views of Travel procedures instead AEO 29/14. G informs us we may be privately not using any bus. Issued three voucher	DAQ
	6.6.19		SDOS ADADOS ? came to inspect my machine gun mind - DOS was of the opinion that rifles Divisions should convert Amunition dump we have here on mine day approved accordingly Issued Mile Voucher	DAQ
	7.6.19		Had ten for 1 hour and a half visited HQ 182, 183 Bdes Thanked on Brigade for replacement of 18 pr Carriage spore ADOS referred to the log BOC wire SC RA re Supplies of B Supplies to horses charge spares to OC BOC replaced the C.P. wagon to last one weft 7.3.	DAQ

T2134. Wt. W708—776. 500000. 4/15. Sir J. C. & S.

WAR DIARY or INTELLIGENCE SUMMARY

Army Form C. 2118.

JUNE
DADOS
61 DIVISION

3

Place	Date	Hour	Summary of Events and Information	Remarks and references to Appendices
LAMBRES	7 & 8		7 & 8 June. General then carried from Nepe.	9920
	13		13 June. Journeyed to interview officials. Travelled from Lopt Boyd served to Find Divisional H.Q. and to interview with G.S.P 16 to discuss Corps and 187 Bath 16 to discuss Corps matters. Mornings of order Div attendant for the use that G Point of Nieppe S. All pieces in action with attachment through tunnel followings in my bearers shop.	
			(A.O.B.) Arrived at 2 p.m. and matters discussed of Appreciation by Brig Gen Heathings of positions [illegible] 6, S/Lieut Reed S/Capt Clement, M/Cpl Grab, who arranged to convene [illegible] 1"×1½ feet from H.Q. to contribute attached with to Corps line and A.O.Q. H.S. repeated my attachment U.O.D.S. so he has ordered that H.Q. has arrived in light to make us be transfer to nos. Eastbourne Clementines and appointment.	9920
	9		3 June. General Meets Q convo with the nos. Lena travel willm, and the influence for inquiry inquiry to half of Masses men through attendance these attempt.	9920

WAR DIARY or INTELLIGENCE SUMMARY.

Army Form C. 2118.

JUNE. D.A.Q.M.S. 6ᵗʰ Division

Place	Date	Hour	Summary of Events and Information	Remarks and references to Appendices
LAMBRES	10		M.O.T. Conv. & tpt matters. Inv. 4/71 Inf. Bde. 4/6 Inf. Bde. S.C.R.A. Q. it w.	DAQ
	11		Supervised M.P.S. Conv. in 2/307 Bde. 16 Div. Arty. -issue of Orders/rations.	DAQ
	12		Did conv. meet at Lambres. Conv. Q.M. i/c and Staff. General matters.	DAQ
	13		A/DAQMG to front and rear areas. To ..... DAQ meetings. General matters.	DAQ
	14		Conveyance O.C. A/71 Bde. 16 D.A. in various areas of the trenches. Various tpts inspected by DA Qm.	DAQ
	15		Interviewed Capt. Lieut. Gen. T Duncan - spoke to MG+T reference the rear arrang.s & supply of amm. inspection and storage for indaluscalt.. etc. to view - 6 numerals.	DAQ
	16		Inv. A/D.A. Q.M.G. S/71 Inf Bde. Various evening Summary by 2/7 Brownies.	DAQ
	17		Gen. R.Bty. in front line healert murred.	
	18		M.P Carriage for DAQ 16D.A. H.S. Hustings 9/10 16 OR.	DAQ

WAR DIARY
or
INTELLIGENCE SUMMARY

(Erase heading not required.)

JUNE 1918
D.A.D.O.S.
61. DIVISION

Army Form C. 2118.

5

Place	Date	Hour	Summary of Events and Information	Remarks and references to Appendices
LAMBRES	19		General Office working	DAO
	20		Spare 6 R.O.S. by phone during that and arrangement with M.T. for delivery. Triumphs taken up from M. Pat. Completing Emergency Sans. Q informed that 7 duplex lorries came into Hd Qrs	DAO
	21			DAO
	22		Arranged for supply of lorries in lieu with "P.U.O." Evened S.O. 16 D.A. Observance put by wanted by Divisions. Keep to C/301 by D.A.	DAO
	23		Visit to prev purchases by Batteries had transferred to Fd. Sec — B.O. % Telmes returned from leave. Sent letter with fig "P.U.O." for Command Travel clerks	DAO
	24		Cape Anstey Q Services supplied me R.A.O. lines to Divisions movements A.D.O.S in to Roulers camp	DAO

Army Form C. 2118.

WAR DIARY
or
INTELLIGENCE SUMMARY
(Erase heading not required.)

JUNE DADOS - 61 DIVISION

Place	Date	Hour	Summary of Events and Information	Remarks and references to Appendices
LAVENTRES	25		General opening	See
	26		Inspected Army horses in transporting line	See
	27		General Office routine	See
	28		Inspected CRE O. ADOS. trips	See
	29		General Office routine	See
	30		General Office routine	See

Chas Crawley Major
DADOS 61 Division

17

Instructions regarding War Diaries and Intelligence Summaries are contained in F. S. Regs., Part II. and the Staff Manual respectively. Title pages will be prepared in manuscript.

WAR DIARY
or
~~INTELLIGENCE~~ SUMMARY.
(Erase heading not required.)

DADOS
61 DIVISION
JULY 1918

Army Form C. 2118.

Sheet I

WO 27

Place	Date	Hour	Summary of Events and Information	Remarks and references to Appendices
LAMBRES	1		Demanded 18 pdr for C/306 61 DA 18 pdr for A/331 66 DA issued to 56 W'shop. General Office routine	DGC
	2		Saw A Q reference Hot food Containers Demanded 12 from Base. Indents 1320 1321 Guns released by Army 1 from G.P. 1 from 31 Workshop. 3 Tons of General Stores up	DGC
	3		General Office work morning 183 Bde in afternoon. St Omer re purchase of [illegible] etc	DGC
	4		Saw CRA. CRE of McAn Corps morning. GOC's Conference in afternoon. 57 Bicycles from Base and 7 bus [illegible]	DGC
	5		QMs' Blakin, Brooks, Oxford called re indents checked etc. General Office routine. Saw DDOS who asked me to endeavour to run putties repairing shop. Informed him that the puttees that eventually came back to us were not worth the trouble – which we use these for patching and repairing other puttees	DGC
	6		Issued [illegible] Gun to 3G MGC. General Office Touring. 5 Tons General Stores 1 Lorry body for 2/6 [illegible]	DGC
	7		159 Bicycles up and 142 Wheels G.P. Returned these to units. Saw Q reference Surplus and unauthorised Machine Guns in Division. Ord Carriage for 18 pdr o/1 indent 1324 issued to 56 Workshop for A/306	DGC
	8		No [illegible] up. Q informed Div was going into rest on 14th inst at Norrent Fontes. Railhead unknown. 13 tons General Stores up	DGC

D. D. & L., London, E.C.
(A10266) Wt W5300/P713 750,000 2/18 Sch. 52 Forms/C2118/16

Army Form C. 2118.

D.A.Q.Q.S.
61 DIVN
July 1918
Sheet II

WAR DIARY
or
INTELLIGENCE SUMMARY.
(Erase heading not required.)

Place	Date	Hour	Summary of Events and Information	Remarks and references to Appendices
LAMPRES	8		[illegible handwritten entries]	
	9			
	10			
	11			
	12			
	13			

WAR DIARY
INTELLIGENCE SUMMARY.

Army Form C. 2118.

DADOS 61 Division July 1918

Place	Date	Hour	Summary of Events and Information	Remarks and references to Appendices
LAMBRES	13		Marks to troops regarding warning enemy aircraft hostile movements rewards	App
NORRENT FONTES	14		Arrangement with Army Remount and gun stores for working of branch stores and remount with I.C.D. Body for B Lances also 84 wheels. Journey from divl area emergency train No 1. Heavy bridging H4.3 also 2" and 1.5" canvas bags and LT canvas hooks to improvise D.R.O. for remounts.	App
	15		Demi superstructure to 75 Supt Rail recovery to Etaps.	App
			Travel Shelter D.R.O. published & received. A.P's Camp Cmdt. Finer area recon.	App
	16		Emb to H.Q. Corps S1 recently referred scarcity permits hostilities D.D.O.S. questioned App75 expanded categorisation to regain arms withdrawn from hostilities wear surplus to establishment.	App
	17		Mtg. to COO Main concerning equipment of clothing received in Green truck. Repts 30% 30% to h/k to HQ for return of "soft" surrender clothing as h/l shut Army to Q	App

WAR DIARY
or
INTELLIGENCE SUMMARY.

Army Form C. 2118.

DADOS
61 Div. July 1916

Place	Date	Hour	Summary of Events and Information	Remarks and references to Appendices
NORRENT FONTES	18.		Reinforcement and reorganisation of Humvees. Reports of 3 Lorries and 13 cars and empties to establishment in the Corps. General Office content.	QM
	19.		Reinforcement M 3-0-7 for units Amb [unclear] in relief.	
			"D" Coys clothing returned by 61 War Cops - have written up and [unclear] P/S items, acceptance [unclear] up P.I. and to 2/Col [unclear] my [unclear] with items arriving [unclear] for 57 DN.	QM
			3T Tons Clothing up	—
	20		14 Days General Training. General Office routine.	QM
	21			QM
	22		Moved — to new area to bring XV Corps 6 [unclear].	QM
	23		QUARNOIS XV Corps emphases appearances. General routine.	QM
WARDRECQUES	24		Turning Lorries up to General Office work - Ammunitions.	QM
	25		General Office work.	
	26		Instructed XV Corps by [unclear] MR arranged for transport [unclear] to teach "G".	

Army Form C. 2118.

WAR DIARY
or
INTELLIGENCE SUMMARY.
(Erase heading not required.)

Instructions regarding War Diaries and Intelligence Summaries are contained in F.S. Regs., Part II. and the Staff Manual respectively. Title pages will be prepared in manuscript.

Place	Date	Hour	Summary of Events and Information	Remarks and references to Appendices
MARICOURT	27			
	28			
	29			
	30			
	31			
NORRENT FONTES				

WAR DIARY
INTELLIGENCE SUMMARY

D.A.D.O.S. 61 Division AUGUST 1918

Army Form C. 2118

Place	Date	Hour	Summary of Events and Information	Remarks and references to Appendices
NORRENT FONTES	1	-	Moved from Grigny to Morfrecques	990
	2	-	M.T. Party to the Marines Records	990
	3		5 Ton Lorries and Record maintenance	990
	4		Lorries for N.T. hrs in Blanchet's	990
	5		3 Ton General Service account and furnished	990
	6		Office Funds	990
	7		5 Ton General Service Int'g. in N.T. hrs for Gloucester Lorries drivers taught with drivers	990
WITTERNESSE	8		16 pieces Timber up to 61 M.T. Column	990
	9		3 Ton General Int'g. "Quartermasters"	990
	10		D.D.O.S. and A.D.O.S. came	990
	11		Lorries to Pro Box Repairs out from lorries to Carriage 18 pp for a/c 29/7/93	990
	12		2 trips for 2 Lorries Ammn to Berrel F/1245	990
	13		2 lorries Ammn return to Gloucester	990

WAR DIARY or **INTELLIGENCE SUMMARY**

Army Form C. 2118.

D.A.D.R.T. II
G. BRANCH
August 1918

Place	Date	Hour	Summary of Events and Information	Remarks and references to Appendices
WIDDERBROUCQ	14	8 hrs	General Shine up - but water tank receiving up an F12 & advised BAO	SEE
	15		Serviced 7kpr to A/30 F/12 & destroyed engine 16 &Pro A/148	SEE
	16	10 hrs	Sent [illegible] train, repairs & [illegible]	SEE
	17		Went to [illegible] RP to try train in Frog 2/3rd line, Inst train in Frog 2/3rd near end	SEE
		6 hrs	Sent [illegible] train [illegible]	SEE
	18		[illegible]	SEE
	19		Serviced 7kpr to A/146 m F12 48	SEE
	20	3 hrs	Sent Queen Mary 6 hrs with lighting & sound returning to truck in ground at [illegible] returning	SEE
	21		6 train 1/F Fry 18po Coweay nearly up & OF Feeds	SEE

WAR DIARY or INTELLIGENCE SUMMARY

Army Form C. 2118.

B.A.D.D.T. III
MOUNT. DIVISION
August 1918

Place	Date	Hour	Summary of Events and Information	Remarks and references to Appendices
MUDROS-BROUCQ	22.		[illegible handwritten entries]	see
	23.			see
	24.			see
	25.			see
TANNAY	26.			see
	27.			see
	28.			see

WAR DIARY or INTELLIGENCE SUMMARY

Army Form C. 2118.

D.A.D.O.S. IV Division
August 1916

Place	Date	Hour	Summary of Events and Information	Remarks and references to Appendices
TANNAY	29		6 Tons clothing & Stores drawn rec'd divisions	880
	30	13.5	Held conference of Divn mounted officers & Tpt O.C. & Tpt officers. Instructions to E.S.M. Ourances I L kind to Tpt Stores Workshops F in Gr Divres	880
	31		Divnal Ord. returns	

O. A. W. Andrews Major
D.A.D.O.S. IV Division
31/8/16

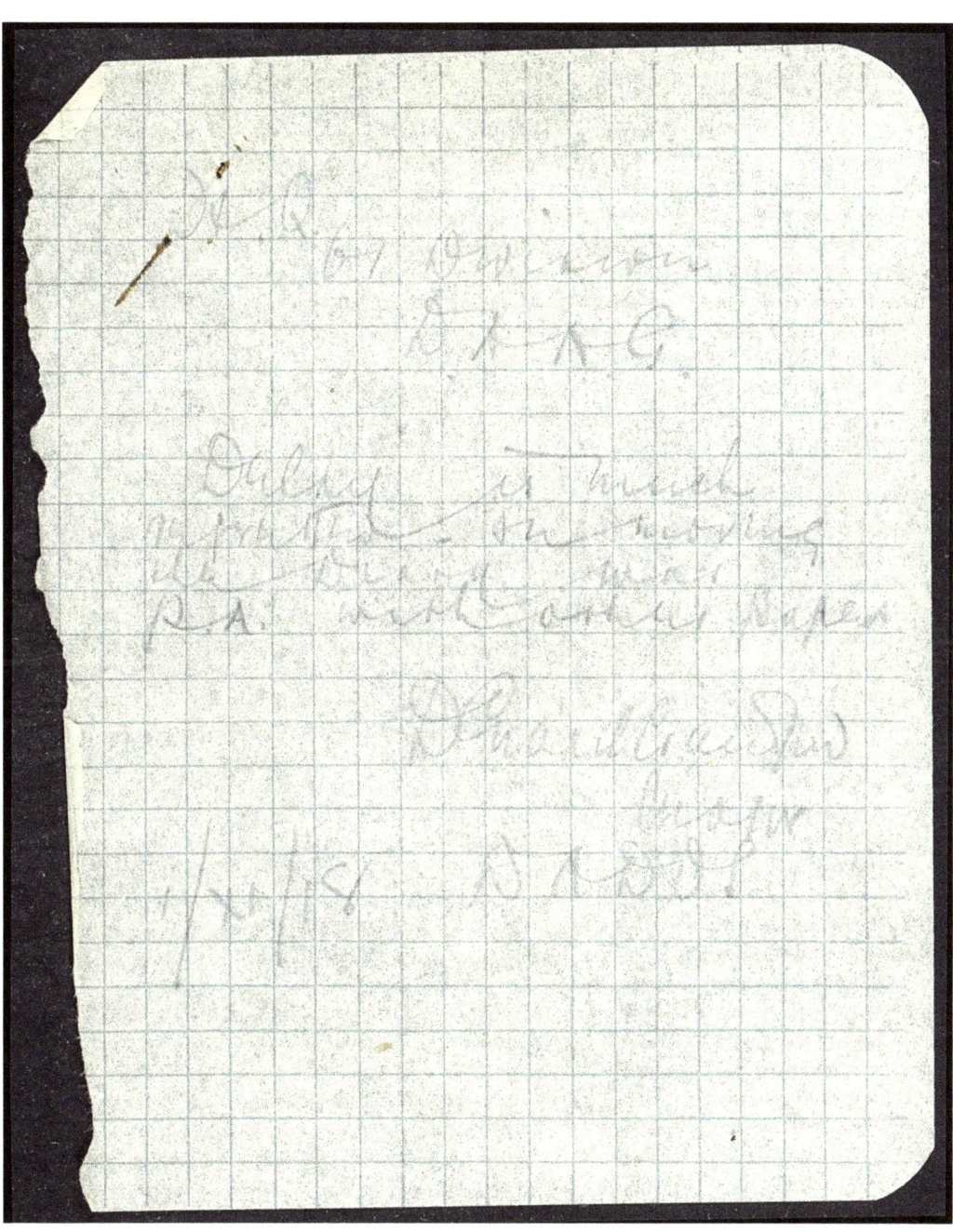

Army Form C. 2118.

WAR DIARY
or
INTELLIGENCE SUMMARY.
(Erase heading not required.)

D.A.D.O.S.
61st Division
September 1918

Place	Date	Hour	Summary of Events and Information	Remarks and references to Appendices
GRIEVE FARM MERVILLE	1		One truck with 4 tons general stores received	
	2		One K.T. Body for 2/7th Oxfords received	
	3		Remained 18 pairs for A Bty 307 Bde	
	4		One truck 6 tons general stores received	
	5		Gen Office Routine	
	6		Demanded Lewis guns for 2/8 Worcester. 5 tons of stores recd.	
	7		A.D.O.S. called. Also A.A. & Q.M.G.	
	8		Demanded Lewis guns for 431st Coy. 4 tons stores recd.	
	9		Demanded K.T. Body for 9th Worcs. Furniture.	
	10		Units stores inspected	
	11		5 tons gun stores recd.	
	12		Visited dump stores dumps	
	13		5 tons gun stores recd.	
	14		4 tons stores received	
	15		Demanded 150 tubs masking for A.D.M.S. (Area 27 ???)	
	16		Demanded 2 Lewis guns for 2/5 Glosters. Recd K.T. Body	
La Gorge	17		4 tons Gun stores recd.	
	18		150 Lachrine buckets recd for Div Area. Demanded wagon cover	
	19		Demanded soft soap for Divl. Trench foot treatment	
	20		5 tons Gun stores received	

Sheet 2

WAR DIARY
or
INTELLIGENCE SUMMARY.
(Erase heading not required.)

Army Form C. 2118.

DROOG 1 Div
September 1918

Place	Date	Hour	Summary of Events and Information	Remarks and references to Appendices
La Forge	21		Visited Salvage Dump. Q.M. Stores received	
	22		5 tons Enid. Stores delivered to Reception Camp.	
	23		A.O.J. Cadu wagon for Signal Coy	
	24		Rec'd Cadu wagon for stores	
	25		Visited Salvage Dump B/30 6 Bde 6 tons stores rec'd	
	26		Demanded 18 pdr for 30 6 Bde. Q.M. Stores rec'd 70 Bdes Stores received	
	27		Demanded 18 pdr carriage for 30 6 Bde. inspected stores received	
	28		18 pdr for B/30 6 received	
	29		5 tons stores received	
	30		Stores delivered to Units.	

A.B.?
Major A.D.?
DROOF 61 Div
30/9/1918

Sheet I

Army Form C. 2118.

ORDOP
61st Div'n

WAR DIARY
or
INTELLIGENCE SUMMARY
(Erase heading not required.)

Army Form C. 2118.

October 1918

Vol 3

Instructions regarding War Diaries and Intelligence Summaries are contained in F.S. Regs., Part II and the Staff Manual respectively. Title pages will be prepared in manuscript.

Place	Date	Hour	Summary of Events and Information	Remarks and references to Appendices
La Forge	1		Wired Cairo to stop issue.	see
	2		All area stores cleared to Corps troops.	see
	3		Cancelled outstanding Indents on firm Park. Indents transferred to Southern Base	see
Arre	4		Wired Havre & Rouen. Can accept stores.	see
Doullens	5		Dumps fired up. Claim sent to 17 Corps & 3 Army.	see
	6		Remained on 3 Army firm bank	see
	7		5000 underwear prs received. Demanded G.S. wagons for D.C.L.	see
	8		Temporary Dump fixed up.	see
Velu	9		100.00 jerkins received. Demanded Drawers & Vests WWB for Div.	see
	10		Dumps fixed up.	see
Gomiecourt	11		Demanded limbered wagon for 61 M.G. Bn. Demanded 3" T.M for 184 T.M.B.	see
	12		A.D.O.S. Called. 6 tons from Havre recd.	see
	13		Stores from 3 Army firm Park received.	see
	14		One from R.T.O transit recd. Stores transferred from truck 24322 to truck 99994.	see
	15		Demanded two Respirators	see
	16		G.S. wagon for D.C.L received	see
	17		Dumps & Office fixed. Location to Corps Army.	see
Cambrai	18			see
	19		A.D.O.S Called.	see
WESNES	20		Demanded K.T. Body for 2/8 Worcesters.	see

Sheet 2

WAR DIARY
or
INTELLIGENCE SUMMARY.

Army Form C. 2118.

DADOS 61st Div.
October 1918.

Place	Date	Hour	Summary of Events and Information	Remarks and references to Appendices
AVESNES	21		Location to Cap. d'Army	
	22		10 tons clothing rec'd from Rouen. Winter from Havre	
	23		Stores rec'd from B Army Gun Park.	
	24		31 tons winter clothing rec'd. Stores received	
	25		one truck of Demanded Vickers Guns for 61 M.G.Bn.	
	26		Demanded Vickers gun for 61 M.G. Bn. Demanded 7 Lewis Guns for 2/6 Warwicks	
	27		500 Magazines received from Gun Park R.	
	28		7 Lewis guns for 2/6 Warwicks rec'd. 2 Vickers Guns for 61 M.G.Bn. Rear.	
	29		Demanded one Vickers Gun for 61 M.G. Bn.	
	30		7 tons clothing from Rouen Rec'd.	
	31		6 tons from Havre 8 tons from Rouen received.	

31/10/1918.

Chaun-Barlow
Major A.D.O.S.
DADOS 61st Div.

Army Form C. 2118.

WAR DIARY
or
INTELLIGENCE SUMMARY.
(Erase heading not required.)

WAR DIARY

November 1918

D.A.D.O.S. 61st DIVISION

Army Form C. 2118.

Sheet 1

D.A.D.S.
61st. DIVISION
November 1918

WAR DIARY

INTELLIGENCE SUMMARY.
(Erase heading not required.)

Instructions regarding War Diaries and Intelligence Summaries are contained in F.S. Regs., Part II and the Staff Manual respectively. Title pages will be prepared in manuscript.

Place	Date	Hour	Summary of Events and Information	Remarks and references to Appendices
AVESNES-LES-AUBERTE.	3		12 lorries General Stores received from Base	926
"	4		Received 9 Lewis Guns for 7th. North Staffs & 2 Vickers for M.G. Battn.	926
"			5 " " for 11th Suffolk Regt.	
"	5		5 lorries General Stores from Above. (Cohuso.)	826
"	6			
"	7		18 pdr. for 6/307 & 18 pdr. for c/307 issued	967
"	8		Railhead changed to G. AUBERTE — one Vickers Gun issued M.G.C.	822
BERMERAIN.	9		Moved to BERMERAIN —	820
"	10		6 lorries clothing rec'd from Base.	830
"	11		Refilled Artillery with 3 lorry loads of Stores at point outside BAVAY.	850
"	12		10 lorries Stores from Above.	880
"	13		18 pdr. for A/307 issued.	890
"	14		Moved Sta. Cambrai.	891
CAMBRAI.	15			897
"	16		3 lorries clothing received. – RAILHEAD changed to CAMBRAI.	899

Sheet 2.

D.A.D.O.S. 61st DIVISION.
Army Form C. 2118.

NOVEMBER, 1918

WAR DIARY
or
INTELLIGENCE SUMMARY.
(Erase heading not required.)

Place	Date	Hour	Summary of Events and Information	Remarks and references to Appendices
CAMBRAI.	20	—	6 tons. General Stores from Base. Indents handed in by Units	App ?
"	21		5 tons Clothing from Base. — One Vickers Gun received M.G.C.	App C
			Indents handed in by Units	App ?
BERNAVILLE.	24		Moved to BERNAVILLE.	
"	28		Kitchen changed to Boulleus.	App ?
"	29		8 tons Horse Shoes Wheels &c received.	App ?
"	30		Blankets (2ww) received from Base.	

D.A.D.O.S.,
61st DIVISION.
No............
Date............

Llewellyn (illegible)
Major A.O.D
D.A.D.O.S. 61st Division

Army Form C. 2118.

WAR DIARY
or
INTELLIGENCE SUMMARY.

(Erase heading not required.)

D.A.D.O.S.,
61st DIVISION.

WAR DIARY

DECEMBER – 1918

2 Sheets

Army Form C. 2118.

D.A.D.O.S.,
61st DIVISION.

Month: Dec 1918

WAR DIARY
or
INTELLIGENCE SUMMARY.
(Erase heading not required.)

Sheet 1

Instructions regarding War Diaries and Intelligence Summaries are contained in F.S. Regs., Part II. and the Staff Manual respectively. Title pages will be prepared in manuscript.

Place	Date	Hour	Summary of Events and Information	Remarks and references to Appendices
BERNAVILLE	4		Received Stour Tickets for Shoko Regt & OR Body for Disly. On.	
"	5		8 Tons Clothing received from Base	
"	8		Moved to ST RIQUIER.	
ST RIQUIER	10		Palliasses received from Base	
"	12		6 Tons Clothing from Base	
"	13		8 Tons from Havre	
"	15		6 Tons Stores from Havre	
"	19		Invoice Clothing from Havre One	
			32 cases Lamps received from Calais	
			12 tons General Stores from Base	
"	21		8 Tons — do —	
"	22		2 Invoice Stores from Base	
"	23		Water Cart Received from Base for 3UL Ambce	

SHEET 2

WAR DIARY
or
INTELLIGENCE SUMMARY

Army Form C. 2118.

D.A.D.O.S.,
61st DIVISION.

Place	Date	Hour	Summary of Events and Information	Remarks and references to Appendices
ROUVER	24		3rd Blankets received from base	
	25		Winter Day	
	27		8000 Ground Sheets from base	
	30		Stores issued to new Units	

M. Kirsch
Capt
D.A.D.O.S 61 Div.

WAR DIARY
or
INTELLIGENCE SUMMARY.
(Erase heading not required.)

Army Form C. 2118.

D.A.D.O.S.
61st DIVISION.

WAR DIARY
JANUARY
1919.

… Army Form C. 2118.

WAR DIARY
or
INTELLIGENCE SUMMARY.

(Erase heading not required.)

January 1919.   D.A.D.O.S. 61st Division

Instructions regarding War Diaries and Intelligence Summaries are contained in F. S. Regs., Part II. and the Staff Manual respectively. Title pages will be prepared in manuscript.

Place	Date	Hour	Summary of Events and Information	Remarks and references to Appendices
St Hilaire	1/1	10	Tons stores received from Base	see
	4/1		18 pdr Ammn Wagon received for 16/307 Bde R.F.A.	see
	9/1	12	Tons stores received from Base	see
	11/1	3	Tons do	see
	13/1	7	Tons General Stores and 12 Tons Vehicle parts received from Base	see
	15/1	*8	pdr Carriage demanded for B/307 Bde R.F.A.	see
	14/1		18 pdr Gun demanded for 16/306 Bde R.F.A.	see
	do		2×18 pdr Guns demanded for A/307 Bde R.F.A.	see
	do		2×18 pdr 21 Carriage demanded for A/306 Bde R.F.A.	see
	do		18 pdr demanded for B/306 Bde R.F.A.	see
	do		4.5 How. demanded for B/306 Bde	see
	do		18 pdr Carriage demanded for A/306	see
	do		18 pdr demanded for B/307 Bde	see
	16/1		1 Tons General stores received from Base	see
	17/1		Kitchen Body (Small) received for 2/4 Oxfds & Bks	see

Sheet 2. D.A.D.O.S.
61st Division

Army Form C. 2118.

WAR DIARY
or
INTELLIGENCE SUMMARY.
(Erase heading not required.)

Instructions regarding War Diaries and Intelligence Summaries are contained in F. S. Regs., Part II. and the Staff Manual respectively. Title pages will be prepared in manuscript.

Place	Date	Hour	Summary of Events and Information	Remarks and references to Appendices
St Riquier	22/1		32 Wheels L.A.S. parts received from Base.	99.Q
	25/1		5 Cane stores received from Base.	99.Q
	28/1		116 Brass throadless received from Base.	99.Q
	29/1		18 pdr remounts for B/305 Bde. R.F.A.	99.Q

[signature]
D.A.D.O.S.
61st DIVN.

"H.Q." 6t Division "A"

Nasmith Meade

Dhani Cautmd
maew
6/1/19   D.H.O.O.

Army Form C. 2118.

D.A.D.O.S.
61st Division
Vol 34

WAR DIARY
or
INTELLIGENCE SUMMARY.
(Erase heading not required.)

WAR DIARY
FOR
FEBRUARY — 1919.

Sheet 1

D.A.D.O.S.
61st Division   Army Form C. 2118.
February 1919

WAR DIARY
or
INTELLIGENCE SUMMARY.
(Erase heading not required.)

Instructions regarding War Diaries and Intelligence Summaries are contained in F. S. Regs., Part II. and the Staff Manual respectively. Title pages will be prepared in manuscript.

Place	Date	Hour	Summary of Events and Information	Remarks and references to Appendices
St Quentin	3	—	6 tons General Stores from Base	&c.
— " —	6	—	8 — to — Genl Rankin	&c.
— " —	7	—	1 × 18 pdr. advanced for B/315 & 1.45 for D/315.	&c.
— " —	10	—	1 tons General Stores received from Base	&c.
— " —	11	—	6 — do —	&c.
— " —	14	—	4 — do —	&c.
— " —	17	—	1 wag. Amm. advanced for D/307 Bae	&c.
— " —	19/20	—	General Routine refitting Artillery Comps.	&c.
— " —	21	—	1 × 4.5 How advanced for B/306 Bde R.F.A.	&c.
— " —	21	—	2 trucks Axes, Picks & Shovels received.	&c.
— " —	24	—	8 tons General Stores received from Base	&c.
— " —	24/28	—	40 tons unserviceable &c Stores sent to Base	&c.

Sect 2.

Army Form C. 2118.

D.A.D.O.S
61st Division
February 1919.

WAR DIARY
INTELLIGENCE SUMMARY.
(Erase heading not required.)

Place	Date	Hour	Summary of Events and Information	Remarks and references to Appendices
Rouen	Feb 26.		3 tons stores from Base & General Routine	RRO

Arwe Curtis
Major R.A.O.C.
D.A.D.O.S 61st Division

WAR DIARY
or
INTELLIGENCE SUMMARY.
(Erase heading not required.)

Army Form C. 2118.

D.A.D.O.S. 61st Division

March 1919.

Place	Date	Hour	Summary of Events and Information	Remarks and references to Appendices
At Rouen	1/3/19.		4 Tons General Stores from Base	See
"	2/3/19.		3 Tons General Stores from Base & One Carter for Co. B'ty 306 B'de	See
"	4/3/19.		3 Tons General Stores from Base & refilled Artillery Group	See
"	5/3/19.		3 Tons General Stores from Base	See
"	12/3/19.		1 Ton General Stores from Base	See
"	"		20 Tons Unserviceable Stores despatched to Base & refilled Artillery Group	See
"	13/3/19.		Transferred 1 W.O. & 1 Storeman to D.A.D.O.S. 19th Division for temporary duty with the 61st Divl Artillery	See
"	"		General Routine & 10 Tons of Unserviceable Stores despatched to Base.	See
"	14/3/19.			See
"	15/3/19.		3 Tons General Stores from Base	See
"	17/3/19.		10 Tons of Unserviceable Stores despatched to Base	See
"	18/3/19.		1 Ton of General Stores from Base & 1 Sergt. 2 Corporals despatched to Le Tréport as advance party	See
"	19/3/19.		Collected 10 Tons of Barrack & Hospital Stores from H.M. Le Tréport	See
"	20/3/19.		" " 10 Tons of " " from E.C.U. Dieppe	See
"	21/3/19.		5 Tons of Unserviceable Stores despatched to Base	See

Army Form C. 2118.

WAR DIARY
or
INTELLIGENCE SUMMARY.
(Erase heading not required.)

March 1919. 2nd Sheet

Instructions regarding War Diaries and Intelligence Summaries are contained in F. S. Regs., Part II. and the Staff Manual respectively. Title pages will be prepared in manuscript.

Place	Date	Hour	Summary of Events and Information	Remarks and references to Appendices
St Riquier	24/3/19		H.Q. 61st Division moved to Le Tréport	APP
Le Tréport	25/3/19		Collected 10 Tons of Barrack & Hospital Stores from R.O.C. Le Tréport	APP
"	26/3/19		" " 5 " " " " from R.O.C. Dieppe	APP
"	27/3/19		3 Tons of General Stores from Base	APP
"	28/3/19		Collected 5 Tons of Barrack & Hospital Stores from R.O.C. Le Tréport	APP
"	"		2.9 Tons of General Stores from R.O.C. Dieppe	APP
"	"		1 Ton of General Stores from Base	APP

[signatures]

WAR DIARY
or
INTELLIGENCE SUMMARY
(Erase heading not required.)

Army Form C. 2118.

APRIL 1919

D.A.D.O.S. 61st Division

D.A.D.O.S.
61ST DIVISION
No.............
Date 7/5/19

Place	Date	Hour	Summary of Events and Information	Remarks and references to Appendices
Le Tréport	1/4/19		2 Tons of General Stores from Dieppe.	
	4/4/19		3 Tons of General Stores from Dieppe.	
	6/4/19		3 Tons of General Stores from Dieppe.	
	7/4/19		1 Ton of Barrack Stores returned to Le Tréport.	
	8/4/19		1 W.O. transferred to G.H.Q. for duty.	
			2 Gunners transferred to No 8 Ordnance Depot for duty.	
	9/4/19		3 Tons of Barrack Stores to Le Tréport.	
	12/4/19		2 Tons of General Stores from Dieppe.	
	12/4/19		39 Bicycles returned to C.O. Le Tréport.	
	14/4/19		3 Tons of Stores from Dieppe.	
	15/4/19		3 Tons of General Stores from Dieppe.	
			2 Tons of Unserviceable Stores to Le Tréport.	
	16/4/19		2 Tons of Barrack Stores to Le Tréport.	

Army Form C. 2118.

WAR DIARY
or
INTELLIGENCE SUMMARY.
(Erase heading not required.)

1st Sheet

D.A.D.O.S.
61st DIVISION.
No. ———
Date 7/5/17

Instructions regarding War Diaries and Intelligence Summaries are contained in F. S. Regs., Part II. and the Staff Manual respectively. Title pages will be prepared in manuscript.

Place	Date	Hour	Summary of Events and Information	Remarks and references to Appendices
Le Tréport	15/4/19		3 Tons Ammunition from Dieppe.	SLC
	22/4/19		9 Tons of Ammunition from Dieppe.	SLC
	"		3 Tons of General Stores from Dieppe.	SLC
	24/4/19		1 Ton of Ammunition from Arnouville.	SLC
	25/4/19		3 Tons of General Stores from Dieppe.	SLC
	26/4/19		3 Tons of General Stores from Calais.	SLC
	29/4/19		3 Tons of General Stores from Dieppe.	SLC

MAY. 1919

WAR DIARY
or
INTELLIGENCE SUMMARY.
(Erase heading not required.)

Army Form C. 2118.

Depots 61 &c 37

Place	Date	Hour	Summary of Events and Information	Remarks and references to Appendices
Le Tréport	2/5/19	2	Tons of General Stores from Dieppe	see
	6/5/19	3	Tons of General Stores from Dieppe	see
	9/5/19	3	Tons of General Stores from Dieppe	see
	-do-	2	Tons of Surplus & w/s Stores returned to Le Tréport	see
	13/5/19	3	Tons of General Stores from Dieppe	see
	15/5/19	2	Tons of Bicycles & Saddlery to	see
	16/5/19	2	Tons of General Stores from Dieppe	see
	20/5/19	3	Tons of General Stores from Dieppe	see
	21/5/19	6	Tons of Box Respirators & Equipment from Abbeville	see
	-do-	3	Tons of Blankets from Le Tréport	see
	23/5/19	2	Tons of General Stores from Dieppe	see
	24/5/19	1	Ton of w/s returned to Le Tréport	see
	27/5/19	1	Ton General Stores from Dieppe	see
	30/5/19	2	Tons General Stores from Dieppe	see

WAR DIARY
or
INTELLIGENCE SUMMARY.

Army Form C. 2118.

JUNE 1919

Place	Date	Hour	Summary of Events and Information	Remarks and references to Appendices
Le Treport	3rd	1 7am	General Stores from Dieppe	920
	6th	2 7am	General Stores from Dieppe	920
	10th	2 7am	General Stores from Dieppe	920
	do	2 7am	Barrack Stores to Le Treport	920
	13th	3 7am	General Stores from Dieppe	920
	17th	2 7am	General Stores from Dieppe	920
	20th	2 7am	General Stores from Dieppe	920
	27th	1 7am	General Stores from Dieppe	920
	28th	3 7am	w/s Stores to Le Treport	920

www.ingramcontent.com/pod-product-compliance
Lightning Source LLC
Chambersburg PA
CBHW081423160426
43193CB00013B/2182